PRAISE FOR THE FBI FILES SERIES

"This page-turning true-crime narrative takes readers behind the scenes of the detailed work, decision-making, and sometimes luck that go into solving difficult cases. The writing is lively, and the principal players are fully dimensional."

—*Kirkus Reviews*

"Denson's well-written, well-researched book engages readers from the beginning and builds suspense as the case hits dead-ends again and again. His lengthy interviews ... supply important background and insight into how they solved the case, grounding this true-crime account firmly in facts."

—*Booklist*

"Denson's text delivers true-crime thrills generally reserved for older readers but packaged here in streamlined content and accessible text, laced with a well-chosen selection of photographs and document reproductions."

—*BCCB*

"The text, pacing, and topic are accessible to reluctant readers, and the back matter features a wide array of resources and additional reading ... An enthralling, well-researched introduction to true crime for upper elementary/middle school readers."

—*School Library Journal*

UNCOVERING
A TERRORIST

Agent Ryan Dwyer and
the Case of the Portland Bomb Plot

BRYAN DENSON

ROARING BROOK PRESS
NEW YORK

For my brothers, Jerry Michael "Dutch" Denson and Cavan Phillip McGregor Denson, who have always had my back. I love you guys.

Text copyright © 2020 by Bryan Denson
Published by Roaring Brook Press

Roaring Brook Press is a division of Holtzbrinck Publishing Holdings
Limited Partnership
120 Broadway, New York, NY 10271

mackids.com

Library of Congress Control Number: 2019948820

Hardcover ISBN 978-1-250-19928-7

Paperback ISBN 978-1-250-19929-4

Our books may be purchased in bulk for promotional, educational, or
business use. Please contact your local bookseller or the Macmillan
Corporate and Premium Sales Department at (800) 221-7945 ext. 5442 or
by email at MacmillanSpecialMarkets@macmillan.com.

First edition, 2020
Book design by Aram Kim

PROLOGUE

Take a close look at the badge on this page.

The shield is gold plated, stands two and a half inches tall, and comes with a solemn pledge. The FBI agents who carry these badges promise to defend the Constitution. They promise to protect Americans from all enemies. They promise to protect us no matter who our attackers might be, and where they might strike.

Fourteen thousand special agents of the Federal Bureau of Investigation, backed by 22,000 support personnel, carry those badges. They work night and day in every state, territory, and corner of the world. They live by the FBI motto: Fidelity, Bravery, Integrity.

In the early days of the organization, America's worst threats were at home. In the 1930s, gun-toting gangsters with names like Al "Scarface" Capone, Charles "Pretty Boy" Floyd, and George "Machine Gun Kelly" Barnes got rich robbing banks, kidnapping children for ransom, and operating illegal bars and casinos. The FBI declared war on these "public enemies," and succeeded in taking many off the streets. But in the last half of the twentieth century, Americans faced new and greater dangers in the homeland.

Highly organized street gangs, the mafia, outlaw bikers, and domestic terrorists became targets of the bureau. The most dangerous were white-supremacist groups such as the Ku Klux Klan. From the civil rights era into the 1980s, those secretive groups terrorized and sometimes killed people of color with fists, firearms, and explosives—and still do even today. By the late 1990s, the FBI declared America's leading domestic terrorist threat to be underground groups such as the Earth Liberation Front, which firebombed businesses and government agencies it accused of harming the natural world.

Then, in a single morning, the FBI's mission changed forever.

On September 11, 2001, al-Qaeda terrorists boarded

four jetliners on the East Coast. Once in the air, they seized control of the planes. In eighty-one minutes, they flew them into the World Trade Center towers in New York, the Pentagon in Virginia, and, thanks to intervening passengers, into a field in Pennsylvania. Those men, on a suicide mission, murdered nearly three thousand innocent people. It was the deadliest terrorist attack in U.S. history—a foreign assault on American soil.

The attacks of 9/11 changed the FBI overnight. Agents still catch bank robbers, kidnappers, and other criminals, but their primary mission today is to protect Americans from terrorists, spies, organized crime, public corruption, cyberattacks, and assaults on our economic, military, and political systems.

Books in the FBI Files series spotlight the FBI's most amazing cases since the bureau began on July 26, 1908. You will meet some of America's worst villains and the heroic men and women who brought them to justice. And you will understand why FBI agents live by the motto Fidelity, Bravery, Integrity.

KEY PLAYERS

The Target

Mohamed Osman Mohamud, an American citizen who came to the United States from his native Somalia when he was three years old

The FBI

Special Agent Ryan Dwyer
Special Agent Miltiadis Trousas
Special Agent Elvis Chan
Special Agent John Hallock
Undercover FBI operative "Youssef"
Undercover FBI operative "Hussein"
Supervisory Senior Resident Agent Nancy Savage

Key Defense Lawyers

Stephen Sady
Steven T. Wax

Key Prosecutors

Assistant U.S. Attorney Ethan D. Knight
Assistant U.S. Attorney Pamala Holsinger
U.S. Attorney Dwight C. Holton

The Judge

The Honorable Garr M. King

A NOTE TO READERS ABOUT
RELIGIOUS TERRORISM

I have studied many kinds of terrorism during my long career in journalism, including those who kill in the name of their religion.

Terrorists calling themselves Christians, Muslims, Jews, Hindus, and Sikhs sometimes turn their faiths into weapons. They twist words of love, forgiveness, and brotherhood into declarations of war. Sometimes they use the words of their holy books to promote hatred in the name of God.

The story that follows of Mohamed Osman Mohamud is not evidence that Muslims are bad people. It is quite the opposite. The great majority of the world's estimated 1.8 billion followers of Islam practice lives of peace, love, and kindness.

I encourage you to practice peace, too. Make the world a safer place. Love your families, your neighbors, and the planet and its creatures.

One day, in a future you can scarcely imagine, your children will thank you.

—*Bryan Denson,*
June, 2020

CHAPTER I

Shortly before lunchtime on July 30, 2010, an eighteen-year-old college student named Mohamed Osman Mohamud walked to a bookstore in downtown Portland, Oregon, to meet a terrorist.

Outside Borders Books, Mohamud phoned the man he knew only as Youssef to let him know he had arrived. The two men had never met, but Youssef instructed him to pretend they knew each other. Mohamud, wearing black pants, a white T-shirt, and a blue fleece vest, stood and waited. Moments later, he spotted a man, in maybe his thirties, crossing the street. In his dark slacks and white button-down shirt, Youssef didn't look like an al-Qaeda recruiter. He could have been any business-man on his lunch break on that warm summer Friday.

The two men had traded encrypted emails for about a week and talked briefly on the phone. Now they were meeting face-to-face for the first time. They greeted each other in English and Arabic, wishing each other peace. Then they walked down the street side by side, making small talk. Mohamud told Youssef he had been born in Mogadishu, Somalia, and was now a student at Oregon State University.

Ten minutes after they shook hands, the two men walked into the Embassy Suites hotel. They found a private alcove off the main lobby and settled into a pair of high-back leather chairs. Youssef got right down to business.

"What have you been doing to be a good Muslim?" he asked.

Mohamud told him he had written articles and poems for a U.S.-based online magazine called *Jihad Recollections*. The publication, read worldwide, encouraged Muslims to rise up against America and the Western world. Mohamud wanted to wage jihad against those who did not follow the word of Islam. Jihad is a word used by Muslims to describe their daily struggle against sin. But Mohamud and those who produced *Jihad Recollections* used the word to describe holy war against

On July 30, 2010, Mohamed Mohamud and a man he thought was an al-Qaeda recruiter chatted privately in the lobby of the Embassy Suites by Hilton in downtown Portland, Oregon. Mohamud said he wanted to take part in a car bombing—perhaps in Washington, D.C. (FBI)

people who rejected Allah (the Arabic word for God). They branded those disbelievers as infidels.

Mohamud posed a question.

"How did you get my email address?"

Youssef calmly explained that a religious council of brothers had passed his name to him. The council, Youssef said, had asked him to reach out to Mohamud and arrange a meeting. Then Youssef asked him a question.

"Can you travel overseas for the cause?"

Mohamud replied that he had once planned to wage jihad in America. But later he had read a Muslim religious text known as a hadith and had a dream. In this dream he had traveled to the mountains of Yemen, a country on the Arabian Peninsula, and trained as a soldier. The dream ended in glory, he said, when al-Qaeda sent him to Afghanistan to lead an army against the infidels.

"That's a very good dream to have," Youssef told him, but "you should probably keep that dream to yourself. We don't know where the *kufar*—the infidels—are. So, we don't want that to get out."

"You know," Mohamud said, "I have some trusted brothers I'd really like you to meet with."

"No," Youssef said, cutting him off. "You know, you shouldn't tell anyone about this meeting. It's for your safety. It's for my safety. You know, the council only sent me to talk to you. It didn't send me to talk to anyone else at this point."

Youssef posed a new question to Mohamud.

"What do you want to do for the cause?"

"I could do anything," he said.

"Look," Youssef said. "I can't put ideas in your mind.

It's got to come from your heart. It's got to come from Allah. So you need to figure out what you want to do."

Youssef offered Mohamud five ways to support the cause. The first was to pray five times a day. This is something that faithful Muslims do every day all over the world. Another way he could help his brothers and sisters overseas, Youssef said, was to earn a college degree, perhaps as an engineer or doctor. He also could raise money for the brothers waging war overseas. Yet another way was to go "operational," meaning attack the infidels. Or, Youssef said, he could become a martyr—someone willing to die in such an attack.

Mohamud spoke right up. He wanted to be operational.

"Well," Youssef said, "when you say 'operational,' what do you actually mean?"

Mohamud said he had heard stories of brothers putting explosives into cars, parking them somewhere, then setting them off remotely. That's what he wanted to do.

Youssef said he might know a bomb expert who could help. He asked Mohamud if he had any targets in mind, and the young man suggested Washington, D.C.

"Well," Youssef said, "have you ever been to Washington? Do you know how to get in and out of Washington?

There's a lot of security around all the monuments and all the places that you would want to target."

Mohamud agreed. He said the towns he knew best were Portland, the biggest city in Oregon, and Corvallis, the town where he attended college.

"Let's finish up this meeting," Youssef said. He suggested that Mohamud think about what he wanted to do. They would have time to discuss his decision in three or four weeks when, if Allah willed it, they would meet again. The two men stood and walked to the hotel entrance, where they said goodbye.

Three hours later, Youssef received an email.

"I have [come] up with a decision about what you asked me to go over and think about," Mohamud wrote. He suggested they talk about it when they met again. Attached to his email were stories he had written for *Jihad Recollections*. The articles were published under his pen name, Ibn al-Mubarak. He had borrowed the name from an Islamic scholar who had lived many centuries before.

Youssef replied two days later.

"Brother," he wrote, "you are talented and [praise be to Allah] I'm very pleased to have met you. [If Allah wills it], we will see each other again very soon." He asked Mohamud if he could count on him to buy a prepaid, disposable cell phone. Criminals often use such phones, known as "burners," so police have a hard time tracing their calls. Youssef wrote that he hoped to get back to Portland soon. And he closed with thanks and his hope that Allah would reward Mohamud's goodness.

Youssef thought Mohamud was probably all talk. Many of the Muslim extremists he came across talked a good game, but their hearts were not cold enough for murder. But Youssef's job demanded that he find out for sure whether Mohamud was serious about carrying out a bombing, because Youssef wasn't really an al-Qaeda terrorist. He was an American citizen born, like Mohamud, in a Muslim nation and raised in the United States.

Youssef was also an undercover FBI agent.

CHAPTER 2

FBI Special Agent Ryan A. Dwyer had listened to the conversation between Youssef and Mohamud through an earpiece. The thirty-six-year-old agent, a kind-faced man with a goatee and the lean build of a long-distance runner, sat in room 426 at the Embassy Suites. The L-shaped room was alive with the activities of other agents who also had listened in on the action three floors below.

Dwyer and another agent, both members of the FBI Special Weapons and Tactics (SWAT) team, would rescue Youssef if Mohamud became violent. They had carried their weapons into the hotel inside normal-looking luggage and now wore military-green body armor that read

"FBI." Dwyer carried a .45-caliber pistol and an M4 military carbine.

Since the deadly terrorist strikes of 9/11, Dwyer and hundreds of other FBI agents had kept tabs on Muslim extremists who spoke of holy war. Few posed any real threat to America. But every so often, the FBI identified and confronted a true believer. Someone like Mohamud. The young man from Beaverton, Oregon, had gone from writing and dreaming about jihad to telling a man he had just met that he wanted to set off a bomb.

"That's pretty extreme," Dwyer recalled. At first the agent figured Mohamud was just another poseur—all talk, and thankfully no action. But later, Dwyer would get the chance to look directly into the young man's eyes. There, he would see a fanatic inspired by al-Qaeda—the terrorist group that had stirred Dwyer to join the FBI.

Dwyer graduated from college in 1996 with no clear view of his future. He joined the Marine Corps and served for four years during a time of peace. When Dwyer's duty drew to a close, he applied to work with the FBI. He thought being an agent would set him at the pinnacle of public service.

Unfortunately, the FBI wasn't hiring.

Dwyer took a job with a high-tech company in California's Silicon Valley, a region in northern California that is the home of tech giants including Google, Apple, and Hewlett-Packard. He earned a good living, but he felt no passion for his work. He missed the Marine Corps. He missed serving his country.

He was getting ready for work on the second Tuesday in September in 2001 when he heard the first reports out of New York. Al-Qaeda terrorists had hijacked four airliners. They had flown two into the Twin Towers of the World Trade Center in Lower Manhattan. The buildings were ablaze. Dozens of people who were trapped in the inferno above where the planes struck chose to leap to their deaths from windows rather than be burned to death. Nearly three thousand people died on that dreadful day.

In the days after 9/11, Dwyer was deeply moved by the story of Father Mychal Judge, a chaplain for the New York City Fire Department. Judge had raced to the Twin Towers to assist victims and pray over the bodies of the dead. After he dashed into the lobby of the North Tower, he was heard praying, "Jesus, please end this right now! God, please end this!" The chaplain was still beseeching God at 9:59 A.M., when he and many others were struck and killed by debris from the adjacent South Tower collapsing in a monstrous gray wall.

"It was the picture of him being carried out of the North Tower that got me," Dwyer recalled. "I was raised Catholic and had seen the selfless dedication of chaplains in the military. Running into harm's way and staying in that chaos in order to deliver last rites and pray for rescuers was an amazing act of courage from Father Mychal."

The 9/11 attack left Dwyer furious and wanting to serve his country again. Al-Qaeda having brought the war to American soil pushed him to reapply for a job with the FBI. The bureau, which historically had served primarily as a police agency, would now focus on protecting national security, and it hired thousands of new employees.

One of them was Ryan Dwyer.

In July 2002, at age twenty-eight, Dwyer began basic training at the FBI Academy in Quantico, Virginia. In a way, it was a bit like going home. The academy and its training ground, some five hundred acres along the Potomac River, sits on a massive Marine Corps base. He had taken officer training at Quantico and been on the base many times.

After Dwyer completed his FBI training there, he spent his first seven years in the bureau's San Francisco division. There, he sharpened his skills as an investigator. He helped convict a gangland killer named Anh The Duong, who had organized a deadly chain of robberies in California and Nevada from 1997 to 2001 in which he shot and killed four people. (Today he resides on California's death row at San Quentin State Prison.)

In July 2009, the FBI reassigned Dwyer to its satellite office in Eugene, Oregon, a town about 110 miles south of Portland. His new boss, FBI supervisor Nancy Savage, put him on the team investigating Mohamud in early 2010. Dwyer had a good reputation, Savage recalled. He had worked well with prosecutors to put criminals such as Duong on trial. He was well organized, she said, and was good on the witness stand when called to testify against the accused at trial.

The FBI had always paid close attention to violent extremist groups. But after 9/11, agents took a special interest in the online talk of Islamic radicals. The bureau paid close attention to their words in hopes of stopping another such disaster.

Agents did not want to prevent people from speaking

their minds. The U.S. Constitution protects Americans' right to free speech. But the FBI sought out people who preached violent jihad or spoke of killing Americans at home or abroad.

Dwyer and many other FBI employees studied the backgrounds of those they thought might pose a threat to public safety. They pored over public records to find out where these potentially dangerous people lived, what kinds of vehicles they drove, what they did for a living, who they associated with, and whether they had ever been in trouble with the law. They read news articles, blogs, and social media sites to see what their subjects were saying in public. When agents identified people who seemed bent on acts of terrorism, they would take action. Using fake names, the agents posed as fellow extremists and reached out to their targets online.

How did they find these people?

Sometimes as they studied social media sites, agents uncovered terrorists behind some of the worrisome content. Other times, the FBI's pool of informants reported possible extremists to agents. Now and again, ordinary people heeded the government's post-9/11 slogan—"If you see something, say something"—and phoned the FBI.

CHAPTER 3

Almost a year before the agent known as Youssef first met Mohamed Mohamud, the FBI took a strange call from Osman Barre, Mohamud's father. (In Somali culture, children typically take their father's first name as their middle name.) Barre phoned the Portland field office on August 31, 2009, and said that Mohamud—brainwashed by Islamic extremists—planned to leave America. He had begged his son not to go. But Mohamud had told him he had his passport and a ticket.

Special Agent Isaac DeLong drove out to meet Barre. The frantic dad, like many Somali American parents, feared his son might go back to Somalia to join the Islamic terrorist group al-Shabab. Barre wanted DeLong to prevent his son from leaving the country. But there was nothing the FBI could do. Mohamud had broken no laws. He had turned eighteen earlier that month, making him an adult. He could fly wherever and whenever he pleased.

Mohamud's mother, who separated from his father that year, also worried that her son would end up in Somalia. Mariam Barre knew a woman whose son had gone back to the troubled East Africa homeland, and she did not want Mohamud to connect with terrorists. Al-Shabab, meaning "the youth," was a terrorist group that appealed to young Somali men who opposed Somalia's government. They followed ancient Muslim laws, such as stoning adulterers, cutting off the hands of thieves, and forbidding men from shaving their beards.

Agents sensed that charismatic extremists had courted Osman and Mariam Barre's son and radicalized him. That evil courtship, playing out online, was a lot like the street gangs that coax children into lives of crime. The agents sensed that Mohamud's parents were good people facing a terrible situation. What they couldn't fully understand was the warfare and strife that had turned the Barres into refugees.

Osman and Mariam Barre had fled a bloody civil war in the Eastern Africa nation of Somalia at different times in the early 1990s. Mohamud, born into this chaos, was just three years old when his mother made her way to Portland. Osman, who had served as a professor of engineering at Mogadishu University, spoke five languages. In Oregon, he proved to be a hard worker, first taking a job on the floor of a bottling plant before working his way up to an engineering job at the Intel Corporation. Mariam, who had labored in the banking industry in Somalia, also found work in Oregon. Friends and associates of the couple would later describe them as good parents who had endured much on their way to becoming Americans. The Barres taught Mohamud and their daughter, born in America, to love their adopted country.

Mohamud, a polite child whose Somali heritage taught him to deeply respect adults, came to be called "Mo Mo." Eileen Wilson, a member of the church that found temporary housing for the Barre family, would later describe to *The Oregonian* newspaper how polite the young Mohamud was. "He kissed my hand every time he saw me," Wilson said. "He would take his shoes off and take my hands and kiss me."

By the time he entered Westview High School, Mohamud was a fully adjusted American—a goofy, fun-loving rapper and writer of poetry. He sometimes skipped classes, talked back to teachers, and earned less-than-stellar grades. But in time, Mohamud buckled down and improved at school. He also grew vocal about his faith, and tried to get non-Muslim friends to convert to Islam.

Classmates would later recall the strange presentation he gave in his junior physics class. Students were supposed to demonstrate the workings of a mechanical device. Some of Mohamud's classmates showed how staplers and other simple gadgets worked, but not Mohamud. He showed the inner workings of a rocket-propelled grenade, a weapon of war.

The last thing Osman or Mariam Barre wanted was for their son to make his way to Somalia. So when Mariam learned that Mohamud had announced plans to leave the United States, she phoned her son immediately. He did not pick up. She left him a message, threatening to go to the FBI. Mohamud returned the call seconds later and his mother soon picked him up at a friend's house. Mariam Barre seized her son's passport, relieved to know he had not bought an airline ticket.

Osman Barre phoned Agent DeLong the next day to let him know everything was okay. He explained that Mohamud had intended to fly to Yemen, where he hoped to attend a religious school and study the Arabic language. Barre told the agent his son had agreed he would not attend the school until after he earned his degree at Oregon State University. Barre then forwarded DeLong an email that Mohamud had sent him, including an attachment about the school: Iman University.

The FBI was already familiar with the university. Its campus, with six thousand students, was a breeding ground for extremists. The school's founder was Sheik Abdul Majid al-Zindani, whom the United States considered a global terrorist. In fact, Zindani served as the spiritual guide of one of al-Qaeda's founders, Osama bin Laden, whom the FBI had branded America's number one enemy.

Though Mohamud's parents had taken away his passport, the FBI took some precautions of its own. The bureau's Terrorist Screening Center secretly put Mohamud on its No Fly List. This meant he could not board any plane in the United States. The list, put together after 9/11, was designed to stop possible terrorists from traveling by air anywhere in the country.

The FBI, as it happens, had been keeping tabs on Mohamud for several months before Osman Barre spoke to Agent DeLong. In early 2009, about six months before Barre first phoned the FBI for help, agents got permission from the secretive Foreign Intelligence Surveillance Court to spy on one of Mohamud's associates: Samir Khan. The twenty-three-year-old American, who lived in North Carolina, was the editor and publisher of the online magazine *Jihad Recollections*. The magazine celebrated Osama bin Laden and al-Qaeda's war against America.

While a senior at Westview High, Mohamud had written articles for Khan under the pen name Ibn al-Mubarak, which Khan edited and published. But Mohamud, then just seventeen years old, had proved too extreme for even Khan. For instance, Mohamud's first article, "Staying in Shape Without Weights," explained the importance of tough workouts to enable one "to damage the enemies of Allah." Before the article's publication, Mohamud sent Khan photos of himself and a friend performing sit-ups, spread-foot squats, and other exercises. They wore long white robes, dark sunglasses, and checkered Arab scarves over their heads to disguise themselves. Mohamud wanted Khan to Photoshop the images so that he and his friend appeared to be working out in front of the World Trade Center towers on 9/11, but Khan had refused. He said the magazine couldn't openly urge people to become terrorists.

Khan later fled America to join the terrorist brotherhood in Yemen. There, he edited a new English-language jihadi magazine called *Inspire*. That slick publication, supported by al-Qaeda, carried two infamous stories by Khan: "I Am Proud to Be a Traitor to America" and "Make a Bomb in the Kitchen of Your Mom." Khan would die in the mountains of Yemen when a CIA drone fired a missile at the car in which he was traveling. Also killed in that September 30, 2011, air strike was another American turncoat, Anwar al-Awlaki, who served as a key religious figure in the Yemeni branch of al-Qaeda.

When FBI agents secretly dug through Mohamud's emails, they found that he admired Awlaki and his video sermons. Many extremists did. "He can sell anything to anyone," a Yemeni official once told *The Wall Street Journal*, "and right now he's selling jihad."

The FBI also uncovered emails between Mohamud and some of his friends. In one note, he complained to a pal in Yemen that during a family trip to England, he had been treated poorly at London's Heathrow Airport because of his name and faith. Mohamud certainly wasn't alone. In the years after 9/11, many Muslims complained that they had been detained by airport security because of their faith or the way they dressed. But Mohamud grew

As a high school senior, Mohamed Mohamud wrote articles for Jihad Recollections, *an online magazine that encouraged Muslims to wage holy war. (FBI)*

boiling mad. He wrote to his friend that the world was full of disbelievers and evil Jews who hated Muslims, and he hoped that Allah would send a group of terrorists linked to al-Qaeda to eliminate those infidels.

Mohamud's emails also revealed to the FBI that he had corresponded with Amro al-Ali, a Saudi citizen who once attended college in Portland. Mohamud had met al-Ali at a local mosque. The Kingdom of Saudi Arabia would later include al-Ali among forty-seven suspects wanted for links to terrorists. Interpol, the global police agency, also named him in a wanted-persons notice known as a Red Notice.

As Agent Dwyer later explained, the FBI tracked al-Ali's movements from Yemen to the northwestern frontier of Pakistan—a region that at that time was thick with operatives of al-Qaeda. Al-Ali and Mohamud had shared emails in code, with al-Ali pretending to be in Saudi Arabia. But he was really in Pakistan, where he was described by Justice Department officials as an al-Qaeda recruiter. Al-Ali invited Mohamud to join him overseas.

A few months after Osman Barre phoned the FBI with concerns about his son, the FBI reached out to one of its best weapons in the war on terrorism—its vast pool of informants. Agents often pay these professional snitches to help them gather information on extremists. The informants' job is to learn what's going on in the minds of would-be terrorists and report their findings to the agents. An informant using the name "Bill Smith" and posing as a Muslim in eastern Idaho reached out to Mohamud online. He wanted advice on how he might join "the fight." But what he really wanted was to see if Mohamud would encourage violence.

Mohamud didn't take the bait. Instead he cautioned Smith to be wary of online "spies."

On December 12, 2009, Mohamud got an email from his friend Amro al-Ali, who wanted to put him in touch with a man who could help Mohamud get overseas. Al-Ali said the man's name was Abdulhadi. He passed Mohamud an email address and password so the men could secretly communicate in the draft folder of the account. Mohamud tried and tried to reach Abdulhadi, but he failed. He had mistakenly typed in the wrong email address.

That error, Agent Dwyer later explained, opened the door for the FBI to find out if Mohamud posed any danger to the public.

CHAPTER 4

On the evening of June 14, 2010, Mohamud's parents drove him to Portland International Airport to see him off to Kodiak, Alaska. A college friend had set him up with a job in the fishing industry. But when Mohamud showed his ID at the security checkpoint that Monday night, blue-uniformed Transportation Security Administration officials told him he could not board his flight.

Osman and Mariam Barre stood with their son on the vast green carpet of the airport concourse. They talked quietly, looking confused. They had no way of knowing that six FBI agents had secretly tailed them to the airport that night. The agents knew Mohamud's No Fly listing would prevent him from boarding his plane.

They also believed Mohamud planned to turn some of the money he had thought he would earn that summer into a plane ticket to Yemen, and ultimately to wage war against the United States.

A federal law passed in the aftermath of 9/11 had made it a felony to support international terrorists. People found guilty of sending money or weapons to such groups, or of joining their fight against U.S. citizens, face up to twenty years in prison—even if they fail in completing those actions. The first jihadist charged under the law was a Californian named John Philip Walker Lindh, who had studied at the same school in Yemen that Mohamud hoped to attend.

In the airport that Monday night, Mohamud and his parents looked up to find two men in business suits walking their way. FBI agents Brad Petrie and Christopher Henderson flashed their credentials and introduced themselves.

"I understand Mohamed was not allowed to fly today," Petrie said, "and we'd like to talk about that if we could."

Mohamud and his parents agreed to join the agents in a Portland police conference room at the airport. They took seats at a long table, where Osman Barre said he was very upset his son had been prevented from flying. He told the agents that he believed his phone call to the FBI the previous summer had put Mohamud in this jam.

The two agents weren't allowed to discuss why Mohamud couldn't fly. Their job that night was to assess Mohamud and try to learn what was going on in his young mind. Petrie asked Mohamud a few questions. Had he ever bought a ticket to Yemen? Did he have any connections there?

Mohamud confirmed that his link to Yemen was a friend from Saudi Arabia, whom he had met in Portland.

"I only know him by Amr," he said.

Petrie already knew about Amr, a former Portland State University student wanted by Saudi Arabia for terrorism. His formal name was Amr Solaiman Ali Alali, but friends called him Amro al-Ali. Petrie played it cool, not wanting Mohamud to know the FBI was investigating al-Ali. He changed the subject, hoping to build a friendly bond with his young subject. He asked Mohamud if he had done anything online—such as looking at violent jihadist websites—that might have put his name on the No Fly List.

Mohamud said he watched sports online, but didn't frequent jihadi websites.

Petrie knew Mohamud was lying, trying to hide his radical side. But Petrie didn't want to tip his hand. His job was over for the night. Mohamud, unable to catch his flight, was allowed to go home with his parents.

Agents could only imagine what he might do next.

On the last Friday in June 2010, the FBI ramped up its investigation.

Special Agent Miltiadis Trousas, assigned to the Eugene satellite office, would take charge of an undercover operation. His goal: find out if Mohamud posed a threat to America. Trousas teamed up with Elvis Chan, who worked on a cyber squad in the San Francisco field office. Chan's unit targeted global terrorists for agents in smaller cities.

Chan and his team of undercover agents and informants often reached out to people in the United States who preached jihad on the internet. These operatives, using phony names, chatted with extremists online. In most cases, they found that the would-be jihadis talked big online, but posed no real danger to the public.

When Chan and his team determined particular online extremists *did* pose a danger, they called upon skilled undercover operatives who posed as Islamic terrorists to get to know the potential threats. These undercover agents, informants, and local police officers were some of the FBI's gutsiest employees, assigned to the FBI's many Joint Terrorism Task Forces. They performed their jobs just like movie stars playing roles.

In this case, Chan called in Youssef, an FBI agent, to find out if Mohamud planned to turn his evil words into evil deeds.

To this day, the FBI will not reveal Youssef's real name. All the bureau will say is that he moved to the United States from an Arabic-speaking nation at the age of sixteen. Youssef joined the bureau in 2004, serving first as a software engineer and later as an analyst. Now, he was a prized undercover agent.

The FBI put Youssef in play just nine days after agents talked to Mohamud and his parents at Portland International Airport. Youssef began by sending Mohamud an email at the secret account his target had used to contact Amro al-Ali. He wanted Mohamud to think he was an associate of al-Ali. His note read, "bro . . . go to hushmail.com and set up an account . . . send a message to me . . . I hope to hear from you soon." Hushmail is an encrypted email service. Because of the secrecy it enables, criminals sometimes use the service. Youssef hoped Mohamud would assume he was a real terrorist trying to hide his identity.

Later that day, Mohamud opened a Hushmail email account. His note to Youssef wished him peace and asked how he was doing. But Youssef did not immediately respond, because writing his reply was a team effort. Trousas and other agents, collaborating over the FBI's highly secure video-chat system, rewrote the note several times. It was crucial for Youssef's reply to sound authentic, as if Youssef was a real al-Qaeda recruiter.

This was Youssef's reply, written partly in Arabic (with translated text in brackets): "[And peace be upon you. Praise be to Allah.] I am good brother thank you for asking. I'm sorry for the delay in our communication, we've been on the move. [May Allah reward you] for responding so soon. Are you still able to help the brothers? [If Allah wills it], I'll hear from you soon."

Mohamud responded later that day.

"i have been betrayed by my family," he wrote. "i was supposed to travel last year but Allah had decreed that i stay here longer than my heart desired. i am trying to find a way to go. i do not think i will [be] able to go for a while. i need to save up and also clear up somethings. look

Salamz brother

From: **Mohammed Mohammed** (　　　　　　　)
Sent:　Wed 6/23/10 1:19 PM
To:　　　　　　　　　　　　　　　

salamz bro...go to hushmail.com and set up an account...send a message to me at
　　　　　　　　　　　, i hope to hear from u soon.

The New Busy think 9 to 5 is a cute idea. Combine multiple calendars with Hotmail. Get busy.

A team of FBI agents carefully chose the wording of an email from an undercover agent to Mohamed Mohamud. The agent, using the name "Youssef," instructed Mohamud to use an encrypted email service so that they could communicate secretly. (FBI)

for my emails [if Allah wills it], i will contact you when i am able to travel. pray for me that allah will free my passage from the lands of [the infidels], peace be upon the messenger of Allah, his family and his companions . . . and peace be to you, and God's mercy."

Mohamud and Youssef exchanged several emails over the next few weeks before picking a date to meet. The Oregon teen invited Youssef to join him at the mosque he attended in Portland, but Youssef flatly refused to meet there. He explained to Mohamud that the infidels had spies in every mosque in America—it was too risky to meet there.

Youssef had other reasons not to meet at the mosque, however. FBI policy forbids agents from entering places of worship to run their operations. Still, agents have at times sent paid informants inside mosques. Not long after 9/11, in fact, an FBI informant named Khalid Mostafa infiltrated a Portland mosque to collect evidence against a group of men who attempted to travel to Afghanistan to fight U.S. soldiers. Mohamud himself sometimes prayed at that mosque.

Mohamud's reply to Youssef revealed that he had concerns. He wanted to know how Youssef had gotten his private email address. Mohamud pointed out that only a couple of Muslim brothers knew that email. He let Youssef know that when they finally did meet, he would have questions. He wanted to make sure *Youssef* wasn't a spy.

On June 26, 2010, Youssef responded: "a brother from oregon who is now far away vouched for you." The agents wanted Mohamud to believe his friend Amro al-Ali had given his private email address to Youssef.

Soon the two men would meet for the first time—an excited teen dreaming of jihad and an undercover FBI agent paid to make sure his dreams didn't come true.

CHAPTER 5

On July 30, 2010, the day Youssef and Mohamud first met at the Embassy Suites, agent Elvis Chan spied on the two men from across the grand, carpeted lobby of the Portland hotel. Chan watched both men take seats in their private spot and begin to talk. But their conversation on that Friday afternoon was hardly private.

Chan wore iPod earphones connected to the walkie-talkie transmitter hidden in his backpack. To anyone passing by, Chan looked like just another middle-aged guy listening to music. But there were no tunes. A microphone hidden on Youssef's body piped his conversation with Mohamud into Chan's earphones.

He was pulling double duty that day. Chan listened to every word uttered by Mohamud and Youssef. But in FBI lingo, he also was serving as primary rescuer. This meant that if Mohamud attacked Youssef, Chan would be the first to jump in to protect his fellow agent. Chan felt keyed up, like a football player ready to enter the game, and he was armed. At his side was a Glock 22 handgun, the FBI's standard-issue weapon at the time. He also carried two spare magazines of .40-caliber ammo in case things went terribly wrong across the room. Tucked into his backpack was a metal telescopic baton, if for any reason he had to knock Mohamud to the floor.

Thirteen minutes after the two men began to talk, Chan was stunned to hear Mohamud tell Youssef he wanted to take part in a bombing. A short time later, Chan watched Youssef walk Mohamud to the door of the Embassy Suites and bid him farewell.

When Mohamud hit the street, an FBI surveillance team tailed him.

"There were multiple purposes for tailing Mohamud," Dwyer later explained. "First, it was about public safety and the safety of the undercover agents. These tails on Mohamud were known as 'pattern of life' surveillance." This was the FBI's way to find out who Mohamud was associating with, and who he might tell about his meetings with Youssef, Dwyer said. "Throughout the investigation, many teams of surveillance personnel were brought in from out of state to tail Mohamud. There were constantly fresh eyes on the target."

The number one goal, however, was to make sure Youssef's cover wasn't blown. If Mohamud had somehow returned to the hotel without agents knowing, they might have seen Youssef hanging out with a bunch of people who looked like federal agents. Surveillance teams made sure that never happened.

After Mohamud left the building, Youssef and Chan caught an elevator to the fourth floor, where they met with the rest of the FBI team to debrief. Every agent in room 426 was shocked by how quickly Mohamud had brought up the idea of setting off a bomb.

The monstrous plan had seemed to come right off the top of his head.

Chan typed up the notes he had jotted down while listening to the conversation between Youssef and Mohamud. He filed an electronic summary of that meeting through the FBI's secure computer network. Then he placed his handwritten notes in a "burn bag" to be destroyed. It was a good thing that Chan typed up the words while they were still fresh in his mind, because the following Monday, the team got bad news. The battery powering the digital recorder had died before the meeting. The FBI had captured not one word of the conversation.

Including Mohamud's comments about detonating a bomb.

On August 11, 2010, Mohamud's nineteenth birthday, he emailed Youssef a poem he had written at the age of fifteen. It was titled "The Dear Martyr Whose Story I Shall Tell." The poem tells of a young martyr armed with an AK-47 assault rifle, killing the infidels.

Youssef read the poem. It was now clear to the agent that Mohamud was more radical than he had thought— and that he had been radicalized for years. He hoped to meet Mohamud again to learn more about his intentions— and this time to record Mohamud's thoughts about blowing up a bomb.

The FBI's assessment of Mohamud was now part of an elaborate sting operation, one of the many investigative tools available to the FBI. Agents are allowed to pose as criminals so they can catch someone breaking the law. But they can't plant the idea of a crime in someone's head and then help them commit it. Agents had to be sure Mohamud really meant to hurt people. Their goal was to get the young man talking and see just how far he was willing to go.

Federal prosecutor Ethan D. Knight, a witty man who looked as if he had been born in a tailored suit, now provided legal counsel to FBI investigators. Knight knew that people arrested in sting operations often claimed that they had been victims of entrapment. This meant they accused police of creating a crime and then pushing them into doing it. It was important for the FBI to capture Mohamud's first words about setting up a bombing. But that ship had sailed when the recorder battery wound down, failing to capture Mohamud's words. So Knight urged the agents to make sure that they recorded the next conversation.

The man to do it was Youssef, who would befriend Mohamud and get him to keep talking. Throughout the sting operation, Youssef would have to convince Mohamud that he was an al-Qaeda recruiter. Youssef would also have to learn everything he could about Mohamud in order to help his fellow agents gather evidence about the proposed terrorist attack.

This would require time and painstaking work, all under pressure. As Dwyer later put it, Youssef's life was potentially in danger and there was no earthly way to know what Mohamud might do next.

CHAPTER 6

On a sunny Thursday evening in downtown Portland, Mohamed Mohamud greeted his new friend Youssef outside the Borders bookstore. It was August 19, 2010, shortly before sundown, the tenth day of the holy month of Ramadan. During Ramadan, Muslims around the world do not eat or drink between sunrise and sunset. Fasting is an important part of their faith; it is a time for worship, self-improvement, and charity.

The two men walked to a nearby Lebanese restaurant and picked up takeout food for three people. They would end their fast after the 8:13 P.M. sunset. Now they strolled into the Embassy Suites, where they made their way to room 927. There, Youssef introduced Mohamud to Hussein, who he said was the al-Qaeda bomb expert he had mentioned in their previous meeting. Hussein, who was in his forties, wanted to hear Mohamud's idea for a bombing.

Like Youssef, Hussein was only pretending to be a terrorist. He was actually a police officer assigned to one of the FBI's many Joint Terrorism Task Forces across the United States. Hussein was ideally suited to play the role of an al-Qaeda terrorist. A foreign-born Muslim who spoke Arabic, he was a gruff, thickset man who projected an air of confidence.

The three men opened the bags of food and broke their fast, a scene secretly observed by the team of FBI agents in the room next door. Agents had hidden tiny microphones and video cameras in Hussein's room. After the foul-up with the previous recording, they knew it was crucial to capture every word Mohamud uttered. They would need those words if they later put Mohamud on trial for terrorism.

Prosecutor Ethan Knight had joined the agents to get a glimpse of their target. He wanted to see if Mohamud would outline plans for a terrorist attack. Knight knew that building a criminal case against Mohamud would require him to prove that the young man had thought about a bombing before the FBI operatives entered his

FBI surveillance teams kept eyes on Mohamed Mohamud as he met with an undercover agent at restaurants and hotels in downtown Portland. (FBI)

life. Hussein, sitting with Mohamud next door, was the first to raise the subject.

"How long have you been thinking about this?" Hussein asked.

Mohamud, clearly trying to impress the al-Qaeda bomb maker, spoke right up. He told Hussein that he had been thinking about jihad since he was fifteen. He explained that he had read about the glory that comes with dying in the name of Allah. Mohamud believed that martyrs were given a special place in heaven. Now, sounding like an eager teen at a job interview, he said that once he had heard about the martyrs, he hadn't needed to hear anything else. That was what he wanted to be.

Dwyer, heavily armed and wearing military-green tactical gear, listened from the next room. Now it was his turn to be stunned by Mohamud's swagger. It seemed to Dwyer that the man didn't want to be just a helper to the two men posing as jihadists—he wanted to be a contributor.

Mohamud told his new friends that he had thought about mounting an attack similar to one that rocked Mumbai, India, in November 2008. In that attack, a terrorist group said to be founded in 1987 with funding by Osama bin Laden, stormed into buildings with military rifles. They killed 166 people, including six police officers. Nine of the attackers died as martyrs.

Now Mohamud told Hussein the story he had previously shared with Youssef about his dream, the one about leading an army in Afghanistan against the infidels.

Hussein took it all in, then spoke directly to Mohamud. "What can I do for you?"

Mohamud spoke with great excitement, words tumbling out of his mouth so fast that Hussein couldn't catch them all. But he did hear the teenager mention a car or truck and the word "*mutafajirat*"—an Arabic word for an explosive device. Hussein shifted uncomfortably in his seat, pretending he hadn't understood what Mohamud was trying to tell him.

"I'd be glad to sell you a truck," Hussein said.

"No," Mohamud said. "I want it for something else."

Mohamud asked Hussein if he had ever heard of Pioneer Courthouse Square. This was an open-air brick amphitheater that covered an entire city block in downtown Portland. It was such a popular meeting place that many locals called it the city's living room. Mohamud explained that just after Thanksgiving, the city holds an annual Christmas tree lighting in the square.

Hussein said he knew nothing about the place.

Mohamud said the square would be a good target. On November 26 at about 5 P.M., he said, a towering Christmas tree would be lighted before a cheering crowd of at least fifteen thousand people—all of them potential victims of a bombing.

Hussein gave Mohamud a serious look. "How do you feel?" he asked.

Mohamud spoke of dying as a martyr in an explosive act of jihad.

In the next room, Agent Dwyer could scarcely believe his ears.

"It was chilling," he said. Here was Mohamud, expressing a desire to be a suicide-bombing terrorist in front of two men he thought were terrorists. "It was definitely shocking," Dwyer said. "Sort of jaw-dropping. *He really just said that?*" Dwyer had no reason to doubt Mohamud's sincerity. Prosecutor Ethan Knight, also in the room, had instructed the undercover agents to give Mohamud some chances to back out of such a monstrous plan. "We wanted to test him," Knight said. "We wanted to see if he was all talk, or if he meant it."

Mohamud told the two undercover operatives that he intended to die in the attack. Because if he didn't, he said, the U.S. government would always be looking for him.

His declaration of his intention to become a martyr at the city square had come just thirty-four minutes into his conversation with Youssef and Hussein. The two undercover operatives held their composure. Calmly they explained to Mohamud that bombing the square would be difficult. They urged the young man to reconsider. They told him there were so many other things he could do for the cause. They told him—just as Youssef had in their first meeting—the many ways he could be a faithful servant of Allah without ever blowing up a bomb.

"There's no shame," Hussein said, "to walk away from this."

Mohamud told the men he was thinking about driving a van loaded with a bomb into the crowd of Christmas revelers.

Youssef got up from his seat and walked toward Mohamud. He stood over him, commanding the young man's attention. A part of him hoped to scare some sense into Mohamud. He told him that he spoke of mass murder as if he were eating ice cream.

"What's in your heart?" Youssef asked. "You know there's going to be a lot of children there?"

"Yeah," Mohamud said. "I mean, that's what I'm looking for." He explained that seeing the bodies of Allah's enemies "torn everywhere" would fill him with happiness. Mohamud said the attack might get the U.S. to stop killing Muslims abroad. He told them that he agreed with "Sheikh Osama" bin Laden, who pushed for terrorist strikes to be carried out on U.S. soil to rob Americans of their sense of security.

Mohamud, as determined as ever, now told the

undercover agents that Pioneer Courthouse Square was just a few blocks away.

"Well," said Hussein, "let's go look at it."

The three men climbed into a rental car and drove to the square. Like the hotel room, the FBI had secretly fitted the inside of the car with cameras and microphones that recorded everything Mohamud said. Youssef and Hussein also wore body wires. Teams of agents and surveillance specialists—some on foot, others in cars—covered every move they made.

Mohamud and his two friends drove to a spot near the magnificent square. They got out of their car and walked down into the brick-lined bowl. The lights of the city were dazzling, and the sky was ablaze with summer stars. Mohamud stopped them at a gap between two posts. Right there, he told them, was where he would swerve his bomb-laden car into the crowd.

After their walk, Youssef and Hussein gave Mohamud a lift back to his mother's home in the nearby town of Beaverton. On the way, still talking to men he believed were terrorists, Mohamud began to cry. He wept for his friend Daulat, whom he had met in Portland. Daulat, formerly of Uzbekistan, had made his way to Afghanistan. There he had joined the *mujahideen*, the guerilla forces

Pioneer Courthouse Square, an amphitheater in downtown Portland, is sometimes called the living room of the city. (FBI)

who endured harsh conditions in their fight against American soldiers.

The two undercover agents would later recall Mohamud's tears. They were real. Mohamud seemed terribly sad for his friend waging war against America. Yet Mohamud had not shed a single tear at Pioneer Courthouse Square as he plotted the murders of thousands of people.

CHAPTER 7

Youssef emailed Mohamud on August 21, 2010, wishing him the peace of Allah. He let Mohamud know that he and Hussein felt closer to him after their meeting. And he asked Mohamud to say a special prayer for guidance.

"A bomb is a very serious matter," Youssef wrote. "I'm going back to the [council] tomorrow to talk about our conversation. They are going to want to know what the plan is, when you started thinking about the attack and why you feel it is justified. I know the answers to this, but I don't want to talk for you, and I want you to do the [prayer] first. I take what you said very seriously, and I have to be sure that you feel the same. This attack must come from your heart, dear brother."

Youssef hoped to scare Mohamud and give him time to reconsider his plans.

Six days later, Mohamud responded. He wrote that he had performed the special prayer, known as *Salat al-Istikhara*. And when he awoke from the sleep that is to follow the prayer, his faith was sky-high. "So," he wrote, "I see it as a sign [if Allah wills it] that the traffic light is green, LOL."

The email troubled Youssef. He could tell that the prayer, with which Mohamud had sought guidance from God, had only brought him closer to blowing up a bomb.

"Every attempt to get him to contemplate what he's saying, every attempt to scare him, every way out that we've given him, well, he didn't take any of them," Youssef would later explain. "He was not scared."

In fact, he said, Mohamud was excited about his plan, intensely believing that Allah was guiding him into a ghastly act of jihad. Mohamud talked more and more about his deep faith. He spoke so often of God that Youssef and Hussein felt as if the much-younger man was sermonizing to them.

On the last day of August, Youssef received an email from Mohamud. He was letting Youssef know that if they

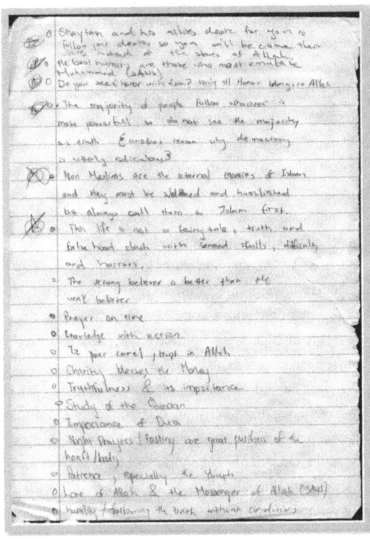

In the pages of a composition notebook, Mohamed professed to love God and the Prophet Muhammad. He also wrote that non-Muslims should be subdued and humiliated but should first be called to Islam. (FBI)

stayed on the right path and worshipped Allah, they would one day reach the highest region of heaven, where they would live like kings.

Mohamud was writing about Paradise, home of the martyrs who suffer or die for their Muslim faith. Islam teaches that suicide is forbidden, but its religious texts say that Allah rewards martyrs for acts of "jihad." Many terrorists have twisted this interpretation to mean that blowing themselves up is not a sin, but rather a ticket to Paradise and everlasting life.

Youssef and Hussein grew worried that Mohamud, so fiercely determined to blow up a bomb, might not wait for November 26 to attack the infidels. They feared he might somehow find real terrorists to help him. "We didn't even want him to think about that," Hussein later recalled. "We didn't know what he would do, who he would get in touch with."

FBI agents take an oath to protect all Americans. This included Mohamud. None of the agents involved in the sting operation wanted to see the troubled teen or anyone else get hurt. Agent Miltiadis Trousas, who was then serving as the day-to-day manager of the Mohamud investigation (thereby bearing the title of "case agent"), knew it would be disastrous if Mohamud somehow mounted a terrorist attack on his own while under FBI investigation.

"We were always on edge during the entire operation," Trousas recalled. "Our main concern was public safety.... We felt Mr. Mohamud was radicalized and dangerous."

For that reason, Trousas gave instructions to Youssef and Hussein: Maintain contact with Mohamud, let him know you are his brothers, and keep building his trust. As Mohamud readied to begin his sophomore year at Oregon State University, about eighty miles south of Portland, Trousas reminded the undercover agents to stay close to their subject.

They had to know what he was thinking.

CHAPTER 8

On September 7, 2010, a cool, cloudy Tuesday in
Portland, Youssef met Mohamed Mohamud at the Starbucks on the north corner of Pioneer Courthouse Square.
They walked four blocks to Habibi, a popular Lebanese
restaurant, and once again bought a takeout meal to
share with Hussein. They carried the food back to a new
hotel, the Portland Marriott City Center, which sat closer
to the square than the Embassy Suites. There, they would
once again break the fast of Ramadan, which would not
end for two more days.

The two undercover agents were on a mission. They
wanted to make sure Mohamud did not take it upon
himself to do anything violent before November 26.

Their plan was to put Mohamud to work. They wanted to see if he would help them build a bomb.

"If he's an active participant in this plan," Youssef later explained, "it will give him a sense of realism. He'll realize—we hope that he'll realize—what he's doing, the magnitude of his plan, and it gives him time to reconsider."

At the Marriott, Mohamud and Youssef took an elevator up to the ninth floor, where they met Hussein in room 902. They waited until sundown to break out their takeout food. The two undercover operatives remained in their roles as al-Qaeda terrorists. They had built a friendly relationship with Mohamud, praying with him and peppering him with praise. It was clear that he looked up to them.

Next door, in room 903, Agents Dwyer and Trousas wore headphones and watched video monitors to catch every word of the conversation in the next room. FBI agents and a federal prosecutor filled the room, some standing, some sitting in chairs, others seated on a pair of double beds. The room was littered with Starbucks coffee cups, bottles of water, food from a local sandwich shop and Voodoo Doughnuts. The mood was so intense that there was little conversation. The attention of every person in the room was glued to what was unfolding next door.

They heard Youssef tell Mohamud that he had spoken to the council. Youssef said this panel of learned Muslim men did not want him to blow himself up. The council, he said, believed Mohamud was more valuable to the brothers alive than dead.

Now Youssef confronted Mohamud face-to-face. He explained to the younger man that he had two choices. He could drive a van to the site of the attack and die in the explosion. Or he could park the van, walk a safe distance away, and dial a cell phone to detonate the bomb.

"This is your choice," Youssef said. "It's what's in your heart. We can't tell you what's in your heart."

Mohamud said that dying for the cause, becoming a martyr, required the "highest level of faith." For the first time, he acknowledged he might not have enough faith to be a martyr. Mohamud thought perhaps his time as a sinful American college kid—an amateur rapper who got drunk, smoked marijuana, and was intimate with women—had lowered his faith.

He told Youssef and Hussein he did not wish to die in the bombing.

Agent Dwyer and the rest of the FBI team were greatly

relieved that Mohamud had decided not to go through with the suicide bombing. For one thing, no agent wanted to see a young man with so much potential kill himself. Agents also knew that if Mohamud chose to take his own life in an act of violent jihad, he might do it without their knowledge, killing innocent people. They believed that giving Mohamud some chores, and keeping him invested in a long-term plan, would prevent such a catastrophe.

Youssef and Hussein gave Mohamud chores to see if he was still committed to a bombing. They gave him $2,700 in cash to rent a storage unit and an apartment in Corvallis, a town of fifty-four thousand along the Willamette River best known as the home of Oregon State University. The undercover operatives wanted Mohamud to live alone, and they told him his place would serve as a hideout right after the bombing.

The two undercover operatives also handed Mohamud $110 to purchase electronic items for their bomb. They secretly hoped that handling these—two Nokia 2320 cell phones, a heavy-duty toggle switch, and a nine-volt snap connector—might make Mohamud see how serious things were getting. They cautioned Mohamud to buy the supplies at different stores, saying they did not want an alert salesclerk to see that he was buying parts commonly used in bombs.

Youssef and Hussein told Mohamud about the construction of the bomb. They would use fifty-five-gallon barrels full of diesel fuel and fertilizer. Together, those ingredients create ANFO, an explosive mixture used in "fertilizer bombs." An ANFO bomb had killed 168 people in the deadliest single act of domestic terrorism in U.S. history—the 1995 bombing of the Alfred P. Murrah Federal Building in Oklahoma City.

Mohamud seemed unfazed by all the bomb talk.

Hussein and Youssef let Mohamud know they planned to flee after the bombing, and that he was welcome to join them. They told him they would likely make their way to Yemen. Then, to see how Mohamud would react, they told him what a tough life he would have in the unforgiving Arabian Peninsula.

"I'm praying for that," Mohamud said.

Hussein and Youssef gave the younger man another task. They asked him to find a good parking space close to Portland's Pioneer Courthouse Square where they could park their vehicle bomb on November 26. Mohamud agreed. He told them that when he found a good

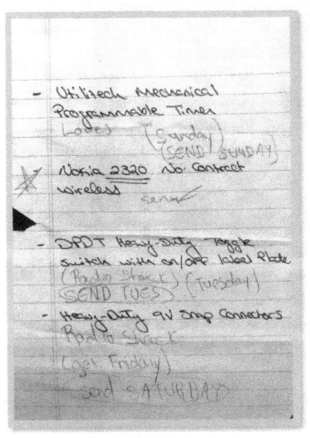

Undercover FBI operative Hussein, posing as a bomb maker, gave Mohamud a list of components to send him to prepare the explosive. Mohamud dutifully bought the parts and mailed them off. (FBI)

spot, he would let them know by email that he had found his "keys."

That kind of sneakiness, recalled Agent Dwyer, showed how resourceful Mohamud had become. He could see Mohamud growing bolder by the day. Coming up with code words like "keys" was a form of criminal tradecraft. Dwyer was now convinced that Mohamud would never back down from the bombing.

"He was not just committed," Dwyer recalled. "He was excited and enthusiastic."

At one point that evening, Youssef pulled out his laptop and showed Mohamud a video of Muslim soldiers at a training camp. They were preparing for violent jihad. But the men in the video, just like Hussein and Youssef, were actors skillfully playing the role of terrorists.

Mohamud watched the video with great interest, unaware it was a fake. Perhaps he saw his own future as a guerrilla fighter, because the video amped him up. He compressed his thoughts into two words.

"It's beautiful."

Youssef and Mohamud later walked out of the hotel and toward the square. A few hundred feet from Pioneer Courthouse Square, Youssef described what the bomb would do.

"I'm telling you," he said, "when you look at all of this you can park the car probably two blocks this way, or this way, or that way—all of this is going to be gone."

"Really?"

"Yeah," Youssef said.

"Wow," Mohamud said. "Like two blocks?"

"Yeah."

"Wow," Mohamud said. "That's amazing."

Mohamud began the fall semester on September 27, 2010. He was enrolled in the second year of his engineering program and living in a shabby $505-a-month studio apartment just north of Oregon State.

There, alone, he wrote himself lists of things to do to stay on the right path. Key among them was to study hard, pray hard, exercise, avoid the temptations of women, and perform the chores that Youssef and Hussein had given him. He also wrote himself a reminder not to show any of his school friends his radical side.

Mohamud was devoted to Islam, but had turned away from the kindhearted Sunni faith practiced by his family eighty miles to the north. While his friends knew he was a Muslim, none knew how far he had traveled into the darkest corners of his beliefs. Mohamud now embraced a religious theory called Salafi-Jihadism. This was the violent creed of Osama bin Laden and al-Qaeda.

After Mohamed Mohamud's arrest, a team of FBI agents searched his apartment in Corvallis, Oregon. (FBI)

Salafi jihadists feel justified in killing innocent civilians, including other Muslims.

To that end, Mohamud would contact Youssef several times in the weeks before starting school. He wrote an email in code to let him know that he had found a spot to park the vehicle bomb: "brother, finally found my keys! Been lookin for a while. Anyways see you soon [if God wills it]." He also mailed off the Nokia cell phones and other bomb components, all purchased from Radio Shack. He dropped a note and a package of watermelon-flavored gum into this package. The note was intended to disguise the real purpose of the electronics and make it look as if Youssef's mother had mailed him the parts.

"Good Luck with ur stereo system Sweetie," he wrote. "Enjoy the Gum."

CHAPTER 9

On the first Sunday in October 2010, Mohamed Mohamud slipped away from his apartment to meet Youssef at a Starbucks near the Oregon State campus. At 5:45 p.m., the two drove across town to the Hilton Garden Inn, which overlooked the university's football stadium, to meet with Hussein.

As usual, an FBI team was already set up in the room next to Hussein's. But this time, Ryan Dwyer couldn't be there. His wife was due to deliver their second child later that month. He had worked long hours on the Mohamud case—often driving home in the middle of the night so he could wake up with her and their son in the morning—but he wasn't going to miss their baby's birth.

Dwyer knew the case was in great hands. Agent

Trousas had expertly run the undercover operations against Mohamud. "Miltos," as some of his colleagues called him, was a soft-spoken agent with an accent he'd brought to America from his childhood on the dazzling Greek island of Corfu. Trousas had joined the FBI just three years before, after careers in tourism and web design.

He was a quick study and a valuable agent. During his short career in the bureau, Trousas had worked on cases against spies, cybercriminals, and terrorists. He spoke five languages, including Arabic, which made him extremely helpful in the FBI's investigations of Islamic terrorists. But for Trousas and his good friend Dwyer, the Mohamud probe was the biggest case of their lives.

The investigation was based out of the FBI's small office in Eugene, Oregon, which was run by bureau supervisor Nancy Savage. She gave roles in the case to every agent in the office—about ten of them. The case was so secret that they could not disclose any detail to anyone not authorized to know.

None of the agents could understand why Mohamud hated America so much. Trousas was among them. He and Mohamud had both been welcomed to America with open arms. But one of them was now plotting mass murder. Which was why Trousas now sat in the Garden Inn, headphones clamped over his ears, watching a live video feed from a nearby room.

The clock was ticking closer to November 26, and Trousas needed to know if Mohamud still planned to carry out a bombing in Portland. He watched as Youssef and Hussein gave Mohamud additional chores.

They asked him to rent a storage unit big enough to park a school bus in, as Mohamud took notes on a Hilton Garden Inn pad.

"The bigger the better," he wrote.

The undercover operatives asked him to also obtain photos of himself—headshots they could use to make phony travel documents.

Mohamud jotted, "2 passport photos."

Youssef and Hussein asked him to find a remote spot to blow up a practice bomb.

"Open testing area (fields, woods)," he wrote.

Now the undercover agents asked him to scout downtown Portland to find the best parking spaces to park their vehicle bomb near Pioneer Courthouse

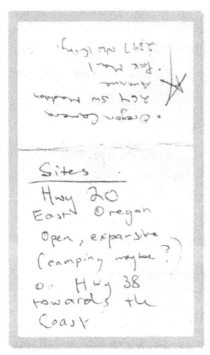

Mohamed Mohamud took careful notes during a meeting with Youssef and Hussein when they met in a Corvallis hotel. His job was to find a remote spot to set off a small bomb—a test explosion in advance of his planned 2010 attack on Portland's Pioneer Courthouse Square. (FBI)

Square. They told him to be sure to find a spot that was as close as possible to the crowds on the night of the Christmas tree lighting.

"I already have it," Mohamud told them.

On a separate piece of notepaper, Mohamud scribbled a big rectangle with the letters "PS" for Pioneer Square. Mohamud pointed out spots along the square to park their truck bomb in.

Youssef and Hussein detected no reluctance in Mohamud. Earlier that month, he had quietly dropped out of college. Now he seemed to be completely at ease mapping out a spot to detonate a massive car bomb. It was clear to everyone watching Mohamud—the undercover operatives and the FBI team secretly looking on—that he was hungry to kill.

Agent Dwyer's wife gave birth to their baby son in October 2010. Now he and Trousas closed in on the final stages of their sting operation.

The two agents spent the week of Halloween 2010 tromping around Lone Spring Mountain in a rugged patch of the Siuslaw National Forest. The FBI had identified the mountain, which rose to 2,519 feet between Corvallis and the Pacific Ocean, as the safest place for Mohamud to detonate a live explosive. Dwyer and Trousas had surveyed the blast site—a steep, dusty hillside covered with the stumps of harvested trees—to make sure no sightseers or elk hunters could wander into the blast zone.

This was their plan: In just a few days, Mohamud would join Hussein and Youssef on a drive deep into the coastal forest. There, the undercover operatives would present Mohamud with a phony but realistic-looking bomb. (Handing a live explosive to a suspected terrorist posed too many risks.) They would place the fake at the edge of the clear-cut and drive to a safe spot several

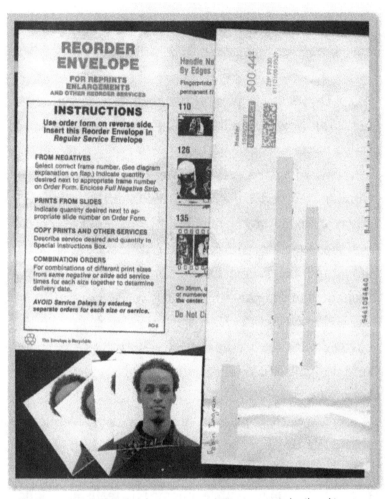

Mohamed Mohamud mailed four passport photos to a man he thought was an al-Qaeda operative. Mohamud believed his friend would use the images to create a passport in the alias he had chosen for his escape: Beau Coleman. (FBI)

hundred yards away. As they drove away from the clear-cut, with their backs to the phony bomb, an FBI agent hiding nearby would snatch the fake, replace it with a real one, and run back to his hiding spot. Then, from a nearby hillside, Mohamud would dial a cell phone to set off the live explosive.

Dwyer hoped the sights, sounds, and smells of the explosion might jolt some sense into Mohamud. Perhaps pushing the keys of a cell phone would trigger more than just a bomb blast—maybe it would awaken him to the horror he planned to inflict upon thousands of innocent people. None of the agents wanted to see a young man with so much promise ruin his life. But their first duty was to protect the citizens of Portland in case Mohamud really did intend to kill them.

Special Agent John Hallock, an FBI explosives expert, had teamed with an Oregon State Police bomb tech to build both the real and the fake bombs. Dwyer was thrilled to have Hallock on the case. Eight years earlier, they had been classmates at the FBI Academy, but the two men couldn't have been more different. Hallock was a force of nature, a big, rugged, friendly agent with a booming laugh; Dwyer was much more reserved. Now, Dwyer would get to see his old friend in action. And

Hallock was "super excited" about it, as he recalled with a laugh. Normally, FBI bomb experts disarm explosives or pick through the wreckage of bombs that have already exploded. Here, he would get the rare chance to blow up a real bomb. "That's what a bomb tech *dreams* about."

Agents planned to record the test bombing from all angles, as if they were shooting a movie. FBI technical agents had rigged Youssef's SUV with hidden cameras and listening devices. They had planted similar electronics on trees and stumps at the test site. But the operation on the mountain was fraught with potential problems. And, they would learn, half the battle would be getting there.

CHAPTER 10

At 2 A.M. on **Thursday, November 4, 2010, Ryan** Dwyer and an FBI sniper took their positions in some brush on Lone Spring Mountain. The sniper wore a ghillie suit, a camouflage outfit that made him look like a heap of forest greenery. Dwyer, who had draped himself with camouflage netting, was there to protect the under-cover agents while also preventing elk hunters or hikers from walking into the blast zone.

There, in the cold, dark, still forest they waited.

At 8:45 that morning, more than twenty miles away in Corvallis, an SUV pulled to a stop near a Starbucks. Youssef was at the wheel and Hussein was in the back. Mohamud climbed into the front passenger seat. Once on the road, the young man pulled a laptop out of his backpack. Photos appeared on the screen, street-view images of downtown Portland near the square. Mohamud had downloaded maps that showed how to get in and out of the city. He also showed the agents the spot he had found to park the vehicle bomb in on the night of the Christmas tree lighting.

Youssef, busy driving, caught glimpses of the screen as Hussein studied the maps with great interest. Hussein applauded Mohamud's attention to detail. The young man had figured out the time and hour at which Pioneer Courthouse Square would reach maximum capacity on the night of the bombing. He was looking for the maximum body count.

Once again, Hussein offered Mohamud the chance to back out. He said that if Mohamud wanted him to vanish from his life and never appear again, he would. But Mohamud, resolute, was all in. Hussein now puffed up his young protégé, telling him that very few people would ever achieve what he was to soon pull off in downtown Portland.

Unbeknownst to Mohamud, FBI surveillance teams in unmarked cars were tailing the SUV, keeping their distance to avoid being spotted by Mohamud. Above them, one of the FBI's surveillance planes kept tabs on the vehicle's movements. At about 10 A.M., agents in the air let FBI teams on the ground know that the SUV had taken a wrong turn. As it happened, Youssef had gotten so distracted by what Mohamud was showing him on his laptop that he had missed a few turns.

At that moment, Trousas and a group of agents and state troopers stood at the intersection of two dirt roads on Lone Spring Mountain. They were there to seal off the mountain from elk hunters so they wouldn't wander into the blast zone. They made up a story, in case anyone should ask, that they had closed the mountain for a training exercise.

But Trousas soon learned to his horror that the SUV was heading their way—instead of on the planned route—and they had to hurriedly move their vehicles off the road. They took cover in some nearby trees, only to learn the SUV was not nearby after all. Youssef, in fact, had gotten them completely lost. The undercover operatives were so far off course that the FBI surveillance plane tracking them nearly ran out of fuel.

At 12:05 P.M., ninety-five minutes behind schedule, the SUV finally reached the test site at the edge of a clear-cut.

Dwyer watched from his hiding spot in the woods as the three men climbed out of the car. He saw Youssef walk away from the others to relieve himself. Hussein then pulled out a cheap blue backpack and lifted out the practice bomb. Mohamud beheld what looked like a small, white, rectangular pillow wrapped with bright orange tape and a striped detonation cord. On top was a clear plastic case that held a Nokia cell phone—identical to those purchased by Mohamud—and a 9-volt alkaline battery nestled in a tangle of multi-colored wires. Hussein now dropped the three-pound explosive into the backpack and set it on a stump.

Mohamud had no clue it was a harmless fake.

Dwyer, still hiding in the woods, saw the men climb back into the SUV. The vehicle moved slowly up a dusty logging road toward a bluff hundreds of yards away. The explosives expert, Agent Hallock, hid near the dummy explosive and watched as the van made its way out of sight.

The FBI secretly prepared one live and one fake explosive for Mohamed Mohamud's test bombing at Lone Spring Mountain. (FBI)

Once he was sure Mohamud couldn't see him, Hallock sprang out of the brush and scurried to the backpack. He replaced the fake bomb with the live one, stuck blasting caps into the explosive, and attached wires to the device. He then unspooled the wires as he walked back to his hiding place. There, he and a state police bomb tech attached the other ends of the wires to a battery-powered switch, which would detonate the bomb when the time was right. Hallock and his partner had practiced this switcheroo so many times that they could do it easily in less than twelve minutes.

A short time later, standing atop the bluff, Hussein held a cell phone in front of him, looking for service. Cell coverage is so spotty throughout much of Oregon's coastal mountains that looking for even a single bar was often wishful thinking. Hussein dialed the number a few times, telling Mohamud he had no success. Then he handed the phone to Mohamud. The young man punched the numbers again and hit the send button.

The phone he called was attached to the dummy explosive, which now sat next to Hallock and his partner. When the cell phone on the dummy bomb lit up, they simultaneously detonated the real explosive.

A powerful blast shook the earth, kicking a cloud of

dirt and smoke high into the air. Grit and pieces of wood debris rained down on the clearing.

Up on the bluff, Hussein shouted that God is great.

"*Allahu akbar!*"

Hussein turned to Mohamud and asked how he felt.

"I feel good," he said. "*Allahu akbar!*"

"That sound?" Hussein said. "Times a thousand."

Hussein and Youssef explained to Mohamud that the test bomb was much smaller than the one they planned to use in Portland. Now Hussein grew serious, speaking to Mohamud as if he were his son. Hussein told him that if he wanted to back out of the Portland bombing, now was the time. But Mohamud declined the invitation to walk away.

"It seems," Hussein would later recall, "that he wanted more."

On the drive back to Corvallis, Youssef asked Mohamud if he would be capable of looking at the bodies of those they would kill on November 26.

Mohamud did not hold back.

"Do you remember when 9/11 happened, when those people were jumping from skyscrapers?" he asked. "I thought that was awesome."

Youssef reminded Mohamud that he would see body parts and blood.

Subject location

Device Location

Undercover FBI operatives Hussein and Youssef took Mohamed Mohamud to a clear-cut patch of Lone Spring Mountain in the Siuslaw National Forest to set off a test bomb. (FBI)

Again, he spoke right up.

"I want to see that," Mohamud said. "That's—that's what I want for these people. I want whoever is attending that event to leave . . . either dead or injured."

Later that afternoon in his Corvallis apartment, still in the company of Youssef and Hussein, Mohamud wrote a script and prepared to make a video.

This was scarcely a home movie. Mohamud wore a camouflage jacket and a bright red-and-white Arab scarf on his head. He had draped himself in a long white robe called a *thawb*—"Sheik Osama style," he said—and knelt on a prayer rug. The video was Mohamud's idea. It was his way of saying goodbye to his friends and family—and taking responsibility for the bombing at Pioneer Courthouse Square, which was just twenty-two days ahead.

Youssef was behind the camera, ready to record Mohamud. Hussein, looking on, was startled by the young man's attire and ingenuity.

"I like it, I like it," he said.

Mohamud cleared his throat, looked directly into the camera, and read his long, rambling statement as the camera rolled. It was a warning to America and its allies.

"A dark day is coming your way," he said. "For as you threaten our security, your people will not remain safe. As your soldiers target our civilians, we will not fail to respond equally. Do you think you could invade us and we would not invade you? By Allah, we have soldiers scattered across the globe."

Mohamud wanted to be one of those soldiers. In his speech, he encouraged his terrorist brothers to sacrifice themselves for Allah. He concluded with a few lines of poetry: "Explode on these [infidels]. Alleviate our pain.

Mohamed Mohamud put on a camouflage jacket to produce a "goodbye" video in his Corvallis, Oregon, apartment. He hoped the video would serve as a claim of responsibility for his planned bombing of Portland's Pioneer Courthouse Square. (FBI)

Assassinate their leaders, commanders, and chiefs. From your brother to his brother, a poem in brief."

Mohamud's plan was to flee the United States before al-Qaeda released the video. He knew that his claiming responsibility for the Portland bombing would be a triumph for his terrorist brothers and make worldwide news.

CHAPTER **11**

Hussein and Youssef drove to Corvallis on November 18, 2010, eight days before Mohamud's planned attack. It was lunchtime when they picked him up and drove to Crystal Lake Storage, not far from the Oregon State University campus. When they reached the business, Hussein asked Mohamud for the four-digit security code he had chosen for the gate to the facility. Mohamud told him he had picked 4255 because it spelled "hajj." This is the name of the annual pilgrimage that Muslims are expected to undertake at least once to visit Mecca, Saudi Arabia, the birthplace of the Prophet Muhammad and the holiest city in all of Islam.

Hussein punched in the code, and the gate opened.

Moments later, the three men opened the big blue

door of the unit, where Mohamud believed that Hussein would build their vehicle bomb. The undercover operatives praised their young comrade for finding a space big enough to secure the vehicle. Mohamud had scouted the massive storage facility in advance, picking it because he observed no surveillance cameras at the property.

The men did not stay long. They climbed back into their car and drove up to Portland. On the way, Youssef asked Mohamud what he would be doing with his life had the three of them not met. Mohamud said he had planned to use money from his summer job in Alaska to fly to Yemen and join the guerrillas.

Dwyer, listening in on the conversation, was satisfied to hear Mohamud confirm that his plans were to wage war against the United States in Yemen. This reassured Dwyer that the FBI had been right to put the would-be terrorist on the No Fly List. He thought that with that move, the bureau might have saved lives—perhaps even Mohamud's life. The guerrillas that Mohamud hoped to join would indeed suffer terribly, with many of them dying in suicide bombings and other attacks.

"He was not a particularly worldly guy," Dwyer later said. "I can't imagine that it would have gone well for him. I think it would have been a short life span."

It was after 3 P.M. when Mohamud and the two under-cover agents reached Portland. They pulled into the Residence Inn, a Marriott property that hugged a wide, muddy stretch of the Willamette River. Inside Hussein's room, Mohamud pulled out his laptop and showed his friends the maps and directions they would need on the day of the attack. Hussein would later recall Mohamud's demeanor on that afternoon, eight days before the attack: "He's excited, can't wait, time is not going fast enough."

It was close to dark when the three men took a drive into downtown Portland. They were soon strolling across the red bricks of Pioneer Courthouse Square. There, Mohamud showed them where the giant Christmas tree would stand, luring thousands of people into the trap he had devised.

"It's gonna be, uh, bait for the fish," he said.

Mohamud also showed the men the parking space at Southwest Sixth and Yamhill Streets where he thought they should place the bomb. He liked that spot better than the others he had identified, he said, because it was next to a rail-car stop. His plan was to buy a video camera to mount above the van's dashboard. That way, on

Undercover FBI operatives posing as al-Qaeda terrorists gave Mohamed Mohamud $2,700 to rent an apartment in Corvallis, Oregon. (FBI)

the ·night of the bombing, they could point the camera lens at the commuter stop and watch video of the scene from a laptop across town. Mohamud wanted to set off the bomb when a train full of passengers had just pulled up, maximizing the number of casualties.

After outlining his plan, Mohamud led his two companions up Southwest Yamhill Street. They crossed the bright lights of Southwest Broadway and made their way to darker streets beyond. There, Mohamud showed them a good spot to rendezvous on the night of the bombing. He thought they should meet outside the Bike Gallery, a popular cycling shop in a town that's crazy about bicycles.

While they were walking and plotting their attack, an FBI team slipped into Hussein's hotel room and plugged a device into Mohamud's laptop that would mirror his hard drive. This would give agents a peek inside Mohamud's cyber life.

The three men ate dinner and drove back to Corvallis. On the drive, Mohamud played a couple of jihadi audios. One featured Osama bin Laden urging Muslims to crush the disbelievers "by jihad, the bullet, and martyrdom."

Before they reached his apartment, Mohamud devised a plan. He and Hussein would wear disguises when parking the vehicle on the night of the bombing, before meeting Youssef at the rendezvous point nearby. He suggested that they wear hard hats and orange reflective vests, making them look like employees of the city's Public Works Bureaus. Mohamud's plan was to park the van in a fifteen-minute space next to the square. There, he said, they would put on their disguises and set orange traffic cones around the van, making it look as if they were on the job.

That way, he hoped, no one would tow the van away.

One day in late November, Agent Trousas walked into an auto rental place near the FBI office in Eugene and told a clerk he needed to rent a large cargo van.

"What do you need the van for?" the clerk asked.

Trousas obviously couldn't tell the man he was an FBI agent—or that the van was going to be the center-piece of a major counterterrorism sting. In Trousas's line of work, sometimes you just have to lie. Agents often mislead people to maintain the secrecy of their investi-gations.

"I have an import-export company," Trousas told the clerk, accentuating his Greek accent. "Olive oil and olives. It's for my business."

Trousas paid in advance for a long-term rental, a white Ford Econoline E-350 one-ton panel van that he believed would serve as evidence against Mohamud. With some work, the vehicle would hold a very large—and utterly fake—explosive. Agent Hallock would build the monstrous device in a secret FBI garage. No one, not even Trousas, knew at that moment that the FBI would later have to buy the van.

On the cold afternoon of November 23, 2010, two days before Thanksgiving, Hussein pulled his car into Crystal Lake Storage in Corvallis.

Mohamud, sitting in the passenger seat, remained electrified about their plans for November 26. He had recently taken steps that would enable him to flee the country after blowing up Pioneer Courthouse Square. He had sent passport photos to the undercover operatives so they could create his phony travel documents. He also had picked the alias he would use to escape: Beau Coleman.

Inside the storage space, the men loaded two fifty-five-gallon barrels, a can of fuel, electrical wires, and a large box of drywall screws into the back of the car. The metal screws, he knew, would be added to the bomb as metal fragments that would fire into the crowd like bullets.

Hussein asked Mohamud to be sure to pick up one more toggle switch that they would need for their explosive masterpiece. The two men would not see each other again until November 26, 2010, which fell on America's biggest shopping day: Black Friday.

Special Agent John Hallock, an explosives expert, built a fake but realistic-looking fertilizer bomb that undercover FBI operatives, posing as al-Qaeda terrorists, presented to Mohamed Mohamud. The dummy explosive was built with six 55-gallon drums that Mohamud believed contained a mixture of diesel fuel and fertilizer known as ANFO. (FBI)

On Thanksgiving Day 2010, Trousas invited Agent Elvis Chan and two other guests—Youssef and Hussein—to feast with his family in Eugene, Oregon. It had been months since they had taken a day off. So, they kicked back, ate turkey, and watched TV as the New Orleans Saints beat the Cowboys in a close one in Dallas.

But for Trousas, the afternoon began on a tricky note. He had to lie to his family about the men who joined them. He made up a story about who they were, and why they had joined the family for the holiday.

At dinner, Trousas's mind wandered. He was fretting about the next twenty-four hours. Years later, he would recall a moment during their Thanksgiving prayers when someone spoke these words: "And God, please always look after us and protect us." Trousas thought of Mohamud and his cold-blooded plan to kill his own countrymen.

"It was a terrifying thought," Trousas recalled. "And I tried to understand why he had so much hate and anger."

At one point on that chilly Thanksgiving, Trousas drew Chan and the two undercover agents into his home library for a private meeting. They played darts, shot pool, and went over their plans for the next day.

"That night," Trousas recalled, "I also thought of how many more Mohamuds were out there trying to manifest their own plans."

CHAPTER 12

On the morning of November 26, 2010, Mohamed Mohamud picked up coffee at a 7-Eleven and rendezvoused with Youssef. At lunchtime, they strolled through a brightly lit Home Depot in Beaverton, Oregon, to buy orange reflective vests and hard hats. Then they climbed back into Youssef's SUV.

They were headed for Portland, and Mohamud's night of infamy.

Youssef later recalled that on the way Mohamud cheerfully described his last twenty-four hours. After Thanksgiving dinner, he had joined friends at the Washington Square mall. Later, the group traveled down Interstate 5 to the big outlet mall in Woodburn, Oregon, to shop for Black Friday bargains. Mohamud's friends would later recount that he was especially free with his hugs, telling them, "I love you guys." Outside the J.C. Penney store, Mohamud ran into a friend he had first met at a Muslim youth camp, and he shared a sip of his Cinnabon coffee, declaring, "I'm having the greatest morning of my life."

The FBI agents secretly watching Mohamud were struck by his clashing personalities. One was the happy-go-lucky college kid, constantly singing and laughing with friends at the mall. The other was a terrorist plotting to kill thousands of strangers with a weapon of mass destruction.

Youssef was keyed up as he steered his SUV toward a downtown hotel. "I knew the day was coming," he later recalled, and that the bomb was a harmless fake. But he grew more and more tense as the hours ticked closer to the Christmas tree lighting. "It almost felt real to me at that point," he said, "because we had done so much planning over the last couple of months. So I was a little on the worried side. . . . I was nervous for Mohamed's outcome."

It's natural for FBI agents working undercover to grow close to the people they investigate. They spend months, sometimes years, getting to know them. Youssef knew that Mohamud looked up to him and cared for him. But he also knew that their friendship, forged by the trickery of the FBI sting operation, was as counterfeit as their bomb.

Youssef's job required him to protect the public from terrorists. He believed Mohamud posed a grave threat to America. So, he performed his role, waiting to see how the day would play out. Perhaps, he thought, Mohamud would back out at the last moment.

"I built a relationship with him," Youssef later recalled, "and we were getting ready to carry out his plan. And today was the day."

Prosecutor Ethan Knight had given Youssef and Hussein specific legal advice: If at any point Mohamud said he couldn't go through with the bombing, the sting operation was over. If Mohamud backed out, the government lawyer told them, they were to take him home.

It was after 1 P.M. when Youssef and Mohamud entered room 733 of the Residence Inn. Hussein had not yet arrived. Youssef lied to Mohamud, telling him Hussein had traveled to the storage center in Corvallis to pick up their bomb-laden van.

Hussein did not arrive until about 3 P.M. The three

men walked to Youssef's car and drove a few blocks to a parking lot where the big Ford cargo van was parked. Together, they got out for a look. Hussein opened a side door, with Mohamud standing next to him. Daylight poured into the cargo area as Mohamud pushed his face inside, his eyes widening as he beheld the bomb for the first time.

What he saw was six 55-gallon drums topped with orange-and-white detonation cord. The drums were lashed together with an orange tie-down cord, making them a six-pack of terror. Wires led from this faux explosive charge to the triggering device, a Nokia cell phone in a plastic case with a toggle switch. Agent Hallock had built the 1,800-pound bomb to fill the cargo area. He also had stuffed rags soaked with diesel fuel into hiding spots in the rear of the van, so the interior of the vehicle smelled of diesel, a key component of a real fertilizer bomb. The device, weeks in the making, looked and smelled terribly real.

This was a test, a defining moment. All Mohamud needed to say was "I can't do this," and the sting operation would end there. FBI agents would have kept close tabs on Mohamud, then gone to see him to discuss his evil intentions. But on that night, Youssef and Hussein could only watch as Mohamud peered at the bomb. They wondered what was going through his mind.

Mohamud spoke just two words.

"It's beautiful."

Agent Dwyer would later view the surveillance images from that moment. The faces of the three men were so telling: Youssef and Hussein looked somber, while Mohamud's face was lit up with a grin.

An FBI surveillance team captured images of Mohamed Mohamud with Hussein (left) and Youssef (right) in the hours before his attempted bombing in downtown Portland. Mohamud did not know the bomb loaded into the back of the van was a harmless fake. The FBI blotted out the faces of the two undercover operatives to protect their identities. (FBI)

CHAPTER 13

In the late afternoon of November 26, 2010, Mohamed Mohamud and the two undercover operatives kicked back at the Residence Inn. They ate slices of take-out pizza and watched TV news broadcasts. One station, reporting live from Pioneer Courthouse Square, estimated that twenty-five thousand people would gather for the Christmas tree lighting.

Mohamud smiled.

When the sun set at 4:32 P.M., he and Youssef and Hussein cleaned themselves in the Muslim cleansing ritual of *wudu*. They washed themselves in the ancient act of purity. Then they spread hotel towels on the floor of the room, knelt on them, and prayed.

That evening, Hussein and Youssef would offer

Mohamud a couple of last chances to back out of the bombing. But he wouldn't hear of it. He was ready, committed.

At about 5 P.M., the three men walked out of the hotel. They climbed into the SUV, with Youssef behind the wheel, and he gave them a lift to the lot where the van was parked. There, they split up. Youssef drove the SUV to the downtown rendezvous spot a few hundred yards from Pioneer Courthouse Square. Hussein and Mohamud took off in the van.

Hussein sat rigidly behind the wheel of the big Ford van, which was moving slowly in the heavy traffic. The strong smell of diesel fuel wafted forward from the cargo area. Mohamud sat in the passenger seat. He heard Hussein, deep in his role as a terrorist, muttering prayers to Allah.

"Do you think there's twenty-five thousand?" Hussein asked.

"Hmm, not yet," Mohamud said. "They'll be there."

Hussein turned onto Southwest Yamhill Street, easing the big white van toward the southeast corner of the square. There, seemingly by a miracle, a car sitting in the fifteen-minute parking spot Mohamud had picked out pulled out of the space, leaving it wide open.

An FBI photographer snapped surveillance images of Mohamed Mohamud and undercover FBI operative "Hussein" as they left a van next to Portland's Pioneer Courthouse Square. Inside the vehicle was an 1,800-pound explosive that Mohamud hoped would kill thousands of people. What he didn't know was that the bomb was a harmless fake secretly built by the FBI. (FBI)

"*Alhamdulillah!* [Praise be to Allah!]" Hussein exclaimed.

"*Alhamdulillah!*" Mohamud said. He told Hussein that their luck was a sign from Allah.

Mohamud did not know that the FBI had choreographed their good fortune. The driver of the car pulling out of the parking space in front of them was an FBI agent. In fact, two agents in different cars had rotated in and out of the space for hours. This was to make sure that when the van approached, Hussein had a place to park. Meter readers, seeing that the cars had been parked for longer than the fifteen minutes they were allowed, had papered both cars with parking tickets.

At 5:19 P.M., with the sounds of Christmas revelers in their ears, Mohamud attached a detonator to the explosive. Hussein powered up the Nokia phone and asked Mohamud to flip the toggle switch. Mohamud pushed it into the "armed" position.

The two men stepped out of the van in their orange vests and reflective gloves. They put on their hard hats. Above them, hidden from Mohamud, an FBI photographer clicked images of the two men strolling casually away on the sidewalk.

At 5:28 P.M., Hussein and Mohamud met Youssef near Bike Gallery. They climbed into his SUV, which moved northward toward Union Station. Hussein continued to mutter prayers to Allah. Youssef told his companions that his legs were trembling. Mohamud looked perfectly at peace.

Just then, Mohamud saw what appeared to be his mom's Volvo near Pioneer Courthouse Square. He pointed this out to his companions and ducked down in his seat. Youssef and Hussein wondered if Mohamud's mother would be attending the ceremony.

"She's not going to the tree lighting," Mohamud reassured them. "That was too close. What are the odds?" The FBI would later determine that Mohamud had been mistaken. The Volvo he saw was not his mother's.

The SUV rumbled on.

"You're almost there," Youssef told Mohamud.

"Now," Mohamud said, "the hard part is over."

Youssef pulled up to Union Station, where the three men said their goodbyes and Youssef walked away. Under the plan agreed upon by the three men, Youssef would escape by train and make his way out of the country. Hussein and Mohamud would head to Mexico and then travel to the Arabian Peninsula.

Now behind the wheel, Hussein drove the SUV to a shadowy parking lot that overlooked the train tracks. They reached the lot at 5:50 P.M.

After months of planning, it was time.

"*Allahu akbar,*" Hussein said. Then, turning to Mohamud, "You ready?"

"Ready," Mohamud said.

Hussein prayed the Shahada in Arabic: "I bear witness there is no god but Allah, and Muhammad is the messenger of Allah."

Hussein handed Mohamud a cell phone. Then the older man, holding a piece of paper, began to call out a ten-digit phone number to Mohamud, still seated next to him in the SUV.

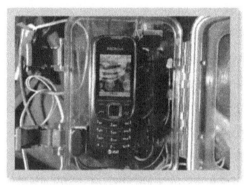

This is a closeup of the cell-phone detonator that Mohamud thought would detonate a massive bomb. (FBI)

At that moment, more than ten thousand people gathered at Pioneer Courthouse Square, waiting eagerly for the moment the Christmas tree would come to life with thousand of lights. The tree stood about one hundred yards from the bomb, which Mohamud, who stood less than a mile away, hoped to blow up in a shower of deadly metal fragments.

Mohamud was so excited to detonate the bomb that he locked his dark, frenzied eyes on the piece of paper in Hussein's hand. He dialed the numbers faster than

Hussein could read them. Then he pressed the send button.

Back at FBI headquarters, a team of agents and federal prosecutors watched a blue light flicker to life on a table, a sign that Mohamud had dialed the number. They waited to see if Mohamud would try again.

Mohamud heard ringing, but no explosion.

"Nothing," he said.

"Hang up," Hussein ordered. "How is the signal?"

"Fine," Mohamud said.

Hussein suggested they both get out of the van and try again. They stepped onto the parking lot. Mohamud then began to dial the number again.

Fifteen feet away, wearing body armor and a blue raid jacket, Ryan Dwyer sat in a van full of other agents and Portland police officers. He wore a transmitter in his ear, awaiting the signal.

At FBI headquarters, the blue light flickered.

Dwyer heard the go code in his earpiece—"Execute! Execute! Execute!"—and leaped from the van. Members of the FBI SWAT team burst out of another van, and a burly agent grabbed Mohamud and took him to the ground. Other agents seized Hussein, who was still playing his role as a terrorist. Hussein, pretending to be surprised, began to shout.

"*Allahu akbar! Allahu akbar!*"

Mohamud struggled against the agents, who pulled his hands behind his back and cuffed his wrists. Subdued, Mohamud looked up to see Agent Trousas and then joined Hussein in his chanting.

"*Allahu akbar!*" he shouted.

Trousas put his face close to Mohamud's and spoke calmly in English and in Arabic.

"*Sadiqi* [my friend]," he said. "Relax. Calm down."

Agents loaded Mohamud into the back seat of a police car, sandwiching him between Dwyer and another agent. As they passed the train station, Trousas, sitting in front of Mohamud, saw Youssef standing outside. Mohamud spotted him too and resumed his screaming. He spat at Trousas and kicked the back of the agent's head with his sneaker. A police detective pulled his Taser gun and fired it at Mohamud, subduing him with a current of electricity. Police quickly bound Mohamud's legs with plastic flex ties.

Moments later, the car descended into the basement of the Justice Center. Inside, Mohamud stood at the booking table, where jailers ordered him to press his fingertips into an ink blotter and then on a piece of paper to collect his prints. Someone put a dark blue garment known as an anti-suicide smock over his head to prevent him from hurting himself. Jailers then sat their prisoner in a chair, instructing him to look up. Mohamud saw a camera high on a wall. A bright flash captured his mugshot, his face frozen in a scowl.

The FBI arrested Mohamed Mohamud on the evening of November 26, 2010, and took him to the Multnomah County Detention Center in downtown Portland. There, wearing an anti-suicide smock, he scowled as a jailer snapped his booking photo. (Multnomah County Detention Center)

In Corvallis, an FBI team searched Mohamud's apartment. They seized his computer, which held al-Qaeda videos and images of some of Portland's past Christmas tree lightings. Agents also found a notebook, one among many, with this notation: "Non Muslims are the eternal enemies of Islam and they must be subdued and humiliated." In the same notebook, Mohamud had written notes to himself. In one, he urged himself to mistrust everyone to avoid the FBI.

Agents in Portland had seized Mohamud's wallet. Inside they found a printed email from Amro al-Ali. The note included Al-Ali's contact information and these words: "Let me know your arrival date." Agents thought this was clear evidence that Mohamud planned to connect with his old friend after he escaped to the Arabian Peninsula. But there would be no escape.

Mohamed Mohamud kept a notebook of reminders as he prepared to detonate a massive bomb in downtown Portland. (FBI)

Mohamud now sat on the floor of his jail cell, under suicide watch, trying to figure out what had happened. A psychiatric nurse came in and sat down across from him, her back against a wall. Mohamud confided in the nurse how important Youssef and Hussein had been to him,

Ten thousand holiday revelers crowded into Pioneer Courthouse Square in downtown Portland on November 26, 2010, for the lighting of a towering Christmas tree. "Little did they know," prosecutor Pamala Holsinger later told a jury, that Mohamed Mohamud "plotted and schemed for several months to kill each and every one of them with a single detonation of a massive truck bomb." (Torsten Kjellstrand, The Oregonian)

and then he wept. He could not understand how he'd gone from being a college student to being someone called a terrorist.

Three blocks away, a towering Christmas tree twinkled brightly on the courthouse square.

CHAPTER 14

Moments after Mohamed Mohamud's arrest, the FBI phoned his father to tell him. Osman Barre hung up immediately and phoned Mariam, his son's mother, who was behind the wheel of her car.

"When you come home, I will tell you something," he said.

"What is it?"

"This is bad," he said.

Osman did not want to break such terrible news to Mariam while she was driving, fearing she would get into a wreck. But Mariam, worried sick, lied to him and said she had just reached her house.

"Mohamed's been arrested," he said.

The FBI spelled out its case against Mohamud in a

thirty-six-page criminal complaint affidavit written by Agent Dwyer. The United States accused him of a single crime: attempting to use a weapon of mass destruction. The charge carried a maximum punishment of life in prison. The arrest made news around the world.

Like anyone else accused of a crime in America, Mohamud was entitled to an attorney. The top two lawyers in the Oregon Federal Public Defender's Office— Steven T. Wax and Stephen R. Sady—jumped in to defend Mohamud. The defense team spent the weekend studying Dwyer's affidavit and talking to their client.

On November 28, 2010, at 2:15 A.M., a police officer in Corvallis, Oregon, spotted a fire at the mosque where Mohamud had sometimes prayed. The blaze that swept through the office of the Salman Al-Farisi Islamic Center had been set deliberately. Someone had broken a window at the mosque, hurling a two-liter soda bottle full of flammable liquid inside.

The timing of the arson, which was a little more than a day after the first news reports of Mohamud's arrest, looked fishy. The attack appeared to be a hate crime that targeted a place of worship, possibly as payback for the Portland bomb plot.

FBI agents poured into Corvallis to investigate. Oregon's

AO 91 (Rev. 08/09) Criminal Complaint

UNITED STATES DISTRICT COURT
for the

District of Oregon

FILED 10 NOV 29 10:33USDC-ORP

United States of America	)	
v.	)	Case No. '10-MJ-497
MOHAMED OSMAN MOHAMUD	)	
	)	
Defendant(s)		

CRIMINAL COMPLAINT

I, the complainant in this case, state that the following is true to the best of my knowledge and belief.

On or about the date(s) of _____November 26, 2010_____ in the county of _____Multnomah_____ in the

_____ District of _____Oregon_____ , the defendant(s) violated:

Code Section	Offense Description
18 U.S.C. § 2332a(a)(2)(A)	Attempted Use of a Weapon of Mass Destruction

This criminal complaint is based on these facts:

See attached Affidavit of FBI Special Agent Ryan Dwyer, incorporated herein by this reference.

☑ Continued on the attached sheet.

Complainant's signature

Ryan Dwyer, Special Agent, FBI
Printed name and title

Sworn to before me and signed in my presence.

Date: _____11/26/2010_____

Judge's signature

City and state: _____Vancouver, Washington_____   Honorable John V. Acosta, U.S. Magistrate Judge
Printed name and title

On November 26, 2010, a few hours after Mohamed Osman Mohamud's arrest, United States Magistrate Judge John V. Acosta signed a criminal complaint charging him with attempted use of a weapon of mass destruction. (U.S. District Court, Portland, Oregon)

top federal law enforcement officials—FBI Special Agent in Charge Arthur Balizan and U.S. Attorney Dwight C. Holton—drove to Corvallis to console fearful members of the mosque and pledge a thorough investigation.

"The fact is," Holton told reporters, "violent extremists come from all religions and no religion at all. For one person to blame a group [of Muslims], if that's what happened here, is uniquely anti-American and will be pursued with the full force of the Justice Department."

Those who prayed at the mosque worried for their safety. Yosof Wanly, the Islamic center's beloved prayer leader, gave thought to moving his family temporarily because he feared retaliation. Mohamed Alyagouri, a father of two, wondered what would stop a hate-filled arsonist from attacking homes or schools. He also feared that teachers or other students might harass his children because they were Muslim.

Eight months later, the FBI arrested twenty-four-year-old Cody Seth Crawford, a self-described "Christian warrior" who ranted against violent jihadists. "If you believe in jihad, you're working for the wrong God. You're a jihadist," Crawford told a police detective. "Muslims are cool. Jihadists are not."

Investigators found Crawford's DNA on a flashlight recovered near the mosque. They found evidence that Crawford had searched the Internet about the Portland bomb plot hours after the first news reports of the crime. On Facebook, Crawford had declared, "That guy on the news used to go to the mosque that is right in frnt (sic) of my house."

Crawford, who suffers from severe mental illness, did not admit he set the mosque ablaze. But in time he pleaded no contest to damaging the Islamic center. Chief U.S. District Judge Ann Aiken sentenced Crawford to five years of probation, a sentence she hoped would get him the mental health care he needed.

Kindhearted worshippers at the mosque reportedly backed the lenient sentence.

People accused of crimes in America have rights.

They are considered innocent until proven guilty. Before trial, police and prosecutors must show defendants all the evidence they have collected against them. This gives accused people a chance to challenge the evidence.

But few criminal cases ever make it to trial in the federal court system. Ninety-seven percent of those cases end in plea bargains. This typically means that a defendant agrees to plead guilty to a less-serious charge in exchange for less punishment.

Mohamud's lawyers, however, would take his case to trial.

On November 29, 2010, the Monday after the Christmas tree lighting, Mohamud appeared in the Mark O. Hatfield United States Courthouse. He pleaded not guilty of attempting to bomb Pioneer Courthouse Square. Afterward, Mohamud's lawyers held a press conference.

Steven Wax told reporters that FBI agents appeared to have manufactured a crime and timed the plot for maximum publicity. Wax could scarcely contain his anger. He said the FBI's undercover employees—Youssef and Hussein—might have coaxed Mohamud into a crime he never would have come up with on his own. Then Wax offered a hint of the legal battle to come.

"The question we'll be looking into," he said, "is the question of entrapment."

Mohamud's legal team hoped to show that the FBI had invented a crime, planted the idea in Mohamud's mind, and then convinced him to do it. The entrapment defense would put the burden on prosecutors: They would have to show that Mohamud was thinking about a terrorist attack before the FBI entered his life, or that agents had not pushed him into the crime.

"Keep in mind we are at the very beginning of a very long process," Wax said to reporters. He pointed out that the FBI had spent fourteen months investigating Mohamud. Now, he said, it was the defense team's turn to look into the fishy tactics of the agents. "The defense investigation," Wax said, "is just getting under way."

America's top law enforcement official, Attorney General Eric H. Holder Jr., declared that very day he was "confident there is no entrapment" in the Mohamud case. Holder said the FBI had given the suspected terrorist many chances to back out of the plot. But Mohamud, he said, had chosen to continue. Senior U.S. District Judge Garr M. King, presiding in the case of *United States of America v. Mohamud*, would later find that Holder's comments violated Department of Justice policy. King noted in a court filing that Holder should have stuck to rock-solid facts, not opinions, and that Holder's comments served no law enforcement function. But he did not muzzle the attorney general. The attorney general decided to wait until after the trial to comment publicly about the case.

King ordered Mohamud to remain in jail as he

awaited trial, saying that he posed a danger to the community and might flee if he were let out before-hand.

FBI supervisor Nancy Savage, who led the FBI's satellite office in Eugene, Oregon, picked Ryan Dwyer to usher the bureau into the trial phase of the Mohamud case. Dwyer would spend two years helping the government lawyers get ready for trial. He would meet with Ethan Knight and fellow prosecutor Pamala Holsinger count-less times, helping them to understand a mountain of FBI evidence. He organized more than thirteen thousand pages of investigative reports, emails, text messages, photos, and transcripts of secretly recorded videos and bugged conversations.

The Mohamud court case, one of the most talked about in Oregon history, would take a couple of years to come to trial. Along the way, King acknowledged that some of his own family members had attended the Christmas tree lighting. But he decided not to recuse himself from the case because he felt he could try Mo-hamud fairly. King also ruled that jurors would be given a guided tour of the big white van, still loaded with the fake bomb. He also ruled that Youssef and Hussein could testify while wearing disguises to protect them from being identified by vengeful terrorists.

So, did Mohamud really plot to kill thousands of people? Or did the FBI cleverly mold him into a monster of their own making?

A jury of twelve citizens would have to decide.

CHAPTER 15

On January 11, 2013, the United States government put Mohamed Mohamud on trial.

Deputy U.S. marshals escorted him into court for opening statements. Mohamud looked nothing like the sullen, angry teen captured in a jailhouse mugshot two years earlier. He was now twenty-one years old. He wore a sweater and dress slacks, his hair cut short. Mohamud smiled at his legal team and took his seat at the defense table, which faced the judge's bench rising from a patch of carpet. He was the ninth terrorism suspect since 9/11 to mount an entrapment defense. The previous eight had all lost their cases.

Federal prosecutor Pamala Holsinger, a former Marine Corps officer, walked across the carpeted floor of

Mohamed Mohamud sat through a three-week criminal trial in the Mark O. Hatfield United States Courthouse, in Portland, Oregon. (Courtroom sketch by Abigail Marble)

the courtroom and took her place at the lectern.

"Ladies and gentlemen of the jury," she said, "this case begins at Pioneer Courthouse Square, [on] November twenty-sixth, 2010," where families awaited the lighting of their holiday tree. "Little did they know that the defendant had plotted and schemed for several months to kill each and every one of them with a single detonation of a massive truck bomb." Holsinger, clutching a cell phone in her hand, told jurors that Mohamud had dialed that phone believing it would set off his bomb. "And when that bomb didn't go off," she said, her blue eyes sweeping the jury box, "he dialed it again."

Holsinger described Mohamud as a man at peace with bloodshed. A man with a violent view of Islam. A man willing to commit chilling acts of violence—even mass murder—in the name of those extremist views. She told them about Mohamud's heroes: Amro al-Ali, whom she described as an al-Qaeda recruiter, and Samir Khan and Anwar al-Awlaki, killed by a U.S. drone strike as Mohamud awaited trial. Holsinger did not mention Mohamud's ultimate hero, Osama bin Laden. Her courtroom foe was about to do it for her.

Veteran defense lawyer Stephen Sady now took his place at the lectern. He was a tall, handsome man, his hair beginning to gray. He had represented a wide range of suspects, from bank robbers to hijackers to suspected jihadis.

"Now, this is a hard case," he told the jurors. He urged them to try the case based on facts and the law, not on fear and emotion. "Because you're going to see pictures, you're going to see videos, and you're going to have emotional reactions to those things," he said. "That's going to be Mohamed there saying harsh things. You're going to see him on video doing bad things." But Sady pointed out that those terrible words and images came after two FBI operatives entered Mohamud's life.

"The fake bomb? That's not going to be disputed," he said. "The fact that Mohamed pushed the cell phone buttons, believing that a huge explosion would occur? Not disputed. That's not the question here. That all happened.

There's also not going to be any question that Mohamed wrote on the internet and spoke with friends about things that are extremely unpopular in this country, about jihad, about al-Qaeda, about Osama bin Laden, about 9/11. It may be that you'll be offended, angry, disgusted at some of the things that you will hear."

But Sady told jurors their job was to answer one question: Did FBI agents target and mold an easily led teen to commit a crime he had not planned or taken a single step to carry out? "In America," he said, "we don't create crime. It's a line the government cannot cross. We all want law enforcement to stop crime. But the FBI cannot create the very crime they intend to stop.

"Mohamed was no terrorist," Sady said. "The

As trial began in the case of United States v. Mohamed Osman Mohamud, jurors asked the judge to provide them a definition of "entrapment." They wanted to be mindful of the possibility that the FBI coaxed Mohamud into a bombing he never would have committed on his own. (U.S. Department of Justice)

FBI just went too far. They created a crime that would never have happened without them. Because the FBI cannot prove beyond a reasonable doubt that Mohamed was not entrapped, the only verdict that can be returned under the law is not guilty. Thank you."

Agent Ryan Dwyer, wearing a dark suit, took the witness stand on January 24, 2013. For the next few hours, prosecutor Holsinger asked him question after question about Mohamud's contacts in the violent world of al-Qaeda.

Mohamud, sitting at the defense table, listened intently as Dwyer told jurors about his contacts with Daulat, the friend who had taken up arms against the United States in Afghanistan. Holsinger allowed jurors to read some of their shared emails on courtroom video monitors. One of the messages, from Mohamud to Daulat, came in the weeks before his planned bombing in Portland. He let Daulat know he was awaiting news of his travels to the Middle East.

Daulat responded: "Brother, while you wait, you should investigate about Predator B, MQ-1 and MQ-9 Reaper striker drones and how to down them." Daulat wrote that some of their brothers who prayed at

Portland's Sunni mosque had science backgrounds and might know how to bring down the drones. "They have killed so many brothers before my watching," Daulat wrote. "By the way, [blessings]. May Allah make you firm on His path."

Mohamud responded nine days before the Christmas tree lighting. He told Daulat he would find him something for the drone attacks, if Allah willed it. Then he warned Daulat not to email him at that address any longer. "If someone replies from now on from this email," he wrote, "it is not me."

This was a clear sign, Holsinger said, that Mohamud expected the FBI to take over his email accounts after he fled the Portland bombing.

Osman and Mariam Barre testified on behalf of Mohamud, describing him as a good son before the FBI—in their opinion—turned him into a terrorist. But jurors probably gave more weight to the testimony of other witnesses, especially a pair of experts on terrorism.

One of the experts that prosecutors put on the stand was Evan Kohlmann, a thirty-three-year-old lawyer and businessman whose security company had collected billions of pages of records on Islamic terrorist groups. Kohlmann testified that he believed Mohamud had wanted to carry out violent jihad years before the 2010 Christmas tree lighting. Defense lawyers introduced Dr. Marc Sageman, a former CIA officer who had interviewed countless terrorists. Sageman told jurors that Mohamud was indeed a terrorist on November 26, 2010. But in his opinion, Mohamud had been only a talker, not a doer, before Youssef and Hussein entered his life.

Perhaps the most devastating testimony came from the two people who spent more time with Mohamud than anyone else from July to November 2010. Youssef and Hussein's blow-by-blow accounts of Mohamud—especially on the day of the attempted bombing—painted a ghastly portrait of a wannabe terrorist.

Closing arguments began on the morning of January 30, 2013, when prosecutor Ethan Knight stood at the lectern.

"Ladies and gentlemen," Knight began, "this case, at its core, is about a choice; a single and remarkable choice, by this defendant, to take the lives of thousands of people he had never met before." Knight told jurors that no federal agent could persuade someone to kill those people and that Mohamud had not been entrapped. "His choice was easy that night, and your choice is easy today," Knight said. "Find the defendant guilty."

That afternoon, Stephen Sady addressed the jury.

"This case is a tragedy," he said. "It's a tragedy for the city of Portland. It's a tragedy for two good parents, Mariam and Osman. And it's a tragedy for Mr. Mohamud. This is a case where the FBI just went too far by taking an action that encouraged tragedy rather than avoided tragedy. The FBI just went too far." Sady condemned the actions of Youssef and Hussein, whom he characterized as the "mentors from hell."

He asked the jury to return a verdict of not guilty.

The jury deliberated for less than seven hours. On the afternoon of January 31, Judge King addressed the panel from his bench.

"Members of the jury, have you reached a verdict?"

"Yes," said juror Daniel Boss.

"Was it a unanimous verdict?" King asked.

"Yes, Your Honor, it was," Boss said.

"All right," King said. He now read Mohamud's fate into the record: "As to the charge of attempt to use a weapon of mass destruction, we, the jury, being duly impaneled and sworn, find the defendant, Mohamed Osman Mohamud, guilty."

Epilogue

A heavy gavel banged loudly on October 1, 2014. Everyone in the courtroom stood as Judge Garr M. King—a slender man of seventy-seven, somber faced, his judicial robes swaying—walked behind the bench and took his seat. That day, King would sentence Mohamed Mohamud for his crime.

King had postponed Mohamud's punishment for nearly two years because of a major legal dispute. Months after the trial, prosecutors had revealed that some evidence shown to jurors had come from a controversial wiretap program. The U.S., with the okay of the Foreign Intelligence Surveillance Court, had learned about Mohamud while eavesdropping on texts, emails, and phone calls of terrorists overseas. Mohamud's lawyers believed this kind of snooping violated his constitutional rights. But Judge King—and later a panel of appellate judges—ruled that the surveillance was legal.

Judgment day began with a ritual as old as the American justice system. King invited Mohamud to stand and address the court, if he wished. And Mohamud rose from his chair looking as somber as the judge.

"The things that I said and did were terrible," he said. Mohamud pointed out that he could not bear to hear the words he once spoke about his extremist beliefs. "I know that I can't change what happened. I can't go back in time, even though I wish I could."

Mohamud apologized to his fellow Muslims for the shame he had brought upon them. In a clear and resolute voice, he told the court that Islam is not about terrorism and killing people. And then he sat back down.

His lawyers had asked King to be lenient, giving him a sentence of ten years in prison. Prosecutors had asked King to put Mohamud behind bars for a term of forty years.

Now all eyes were on King, who drew the courtroom's attention back to Mohamud's monstrous plan for the thousands of people, including members of King's own family, who were gathered at Pioneer Courthouse Square on that drizzly night in 2010.

"He wanted everyone to leave either dead or injured," King said. "This sentence needs to be long enough to deter other potential terrorists."

King imposed a sentence of thirty years.

"This is a very sad case," he said. "I recognize that it is a very long sentence, and I recognize that it's going to be

Jailers in the Multnomah County Detention Center shot a booking photo of Mohamed Mohamud in 2014, the year he was sentenced for the Portland bomb plot. (Multnomah County Detention Center)

some time before Mr. Mohamud will be able to get out of prison and lead a life."

Members of Mohamud's family gasped and left the courtroom weeping.

MOHAMED OSMAN MOHAMUD appealed the verdict in his case, but the Ninth U.S. Circuit Court of Appeals upheld the conviction. Today he lives in a federal prison in Sandstone, Minnesota, as Inmate No. 73079-065.

Mohamud's expected release date is January 26, 2037. He will be forty-five years old.

In 2014, FBI Director James B. Comey Jr. presented key members of the Mohamud investigation team—RYAN DWYER and MILTIADIS TROUSAS, ELVIS CHAN, and undercover operatives YOUSSEF and HUSSEIN with the Director's Award for Excellence in the category of Outstanding Counterterrorism Investigation. The following year, Dwyer and Trousas and ten other key figures in the Mohamud prosecution—including ETHAN D. KNIGHT and PAMALA HOLSINGER—received the Attorney General's Award for Excellence in Furthering the Interests of U.S. National Security.

Putting Mohamud behind bars did more than bring a dangerous extremist to justice, said BILLY J. WILLIAMS, the U.S. attorney for Oregon. "It affirmed the validity of terrorism sting investigations."

The Mohamud case served as a career milestone for Dwyer and Trousas. For Trousas, it marked a new beginning in his career as an agent. Today he travels the world, often working undercover. For that reason, there are no photographs of him in this book.

Dwyer now heads the FBI's satellite office in Eugene, Oregon.

JUDGE GARR M. KING, who presided in Mohamud's trial, died on February 5, 2019, after a long illness. He was eighty-three.

In 2017, the story of the Mohamud case took a peculiar turn.

PRESIDENT DONALD TRUMP signed an executive order that forbade citizens of six majority-Muslim nations, including Somalia, from entering the United States. He used Mohamud's thirty-year prison sentence to justify his travel ban.

Special Agent Ryan Dwyer, a key figure in the FBI sting operation that ended in Mohamed Mohamud's arrest, was a heavily armed SWAT member during meetings between Mohamud and undercover FBI operatives. (Bryan Denson)

"Recent history," the order read, "shows that some of those who have entered the United States through our immigration system have proved to be threats to our national security."

The president used Mohamud, a Somali refugee, as an example. His order mentioned Mohamud's attempt to set off a bomb at Portland's Christmas tree-lighting ceremony.

DWIGHT C. HOLTON, the former U.S. attorney whose office had prosecuted Mohamud, was startled by President Trump's order. "[Mohamud's] radicalization had precisely nothing to do with his refugee status," Holton told a reporter at the time. Indeed, Mohamud was just three years old when he came to America.

More important, Holton pointed out, a Somali refugee had played a crucial role in bringing Mohamud to the attention of the FBI. **OSMAN BARRE**, Mohamud's father, had gone to the bureau with concerns that his son had been brainwashed by extremists. Barre was a good citizen who did the right thing, Holton said, possibly saving his son's life.

"The assistance of the refugee community," Holton said, "was crucial to this investigation."

Author's Note

This book began with a text message.

The note popped up on my phone at precisely 5:52 P.M. on Friday, November 26, 2010. I was sitting at my desk in the newsroom of *The Oregonian* in Portland, Oregon. I was the daily newspaper's federal courts reporter.

"Will need to speak with you in next few hrs," the text read.

The message was from U.S. Attorney Dwight C. Holton, the top federal law enforcement official in Oregon. I knew something was up. Something big. So I replied to Holton, hoping he would tell me what he knew. But he couldn't.

Hours later, inside a conference room in the U.S. Attorney's office, another reporter and I would be the first two journalists in the world to learn some startling news.

Minutes before Holton's text arrived on my phone,

the FBI had arrested Mohamed Osman Mohamud. The parking lot where he was apprehended was less than a mile from my office. There, as you have already read, Mohamud tried to set off what he believed was a live bomb that weighed nearly a ton. Had he succeeded, the bomb would have killed many of the thousands of people gathered at Portland's annual Christmas tree-lighting ceremony.

The story of a teenager trying to kill thousands of innocent people in the name of al-Qaeda horrified Portland and the rest of America. It left me uneasy, too. The newspaper office where I worked sat five blocks from the square.

Holton knew that news reports about Mohamud's arrest, including my own stories, would frighten people. So he had personally attended the Christmas tree lighting. This was to show that the FBI sting operation had put no one at risk.

I spent the next couple of years covering every stage of the USA v. Mohamud case. I became a student of international terrorism and the use of FBI sting operations when those cases emerged on U.S. soil. I toured the jail where Mohamud awaited trial. I remember peering through a tiny window into his corner cell, where he rested on a bench-style bed next to a copy of the Quran. I waved hello, and Mohamud waved back.

Later, I covered Mohamud's three-week trial, often filing two news stories a day on www.oregonlive.com. I knew that the FBI investigation and Mohamud's trial would give readers of this book a rare glimpse inside an FBI sting operation.

I hope the story showed you how far a young man can stray from his good family, and God, and how far he was willing to go to wage war against America. I also hope it shows just how far the FBI will go to prevent a wannabe terrorist from killing himself and thousands of his fellow citizens.

Timeline

February 2009: Mohamed Mohamud, a high school senior in Beaverton, Oregon, begins a six-month email correspondence with Samir Khan. Khan is the young publisher of an online magazine called *Jihad Recollections*. FBI agents in Charlotte, North Carolina, intercept Mohamud's emails to and from Khan (with the permission of the Foreign Intelligence Surveillance Court).

April–May 2009: Mohamud writes two articles for *Jihad Recollections* under the pen name Ibn al-Mubarak. The first teaches Islamic fighters how to stay in shape without using weights. The second, "Preparing for the Long Night," instructs them on how to stay awake as they prepare to ambush the enemies of Allah.

June 2009: Mohamud graduates from Westview High School.

August 2009: *Jihad Recollections* publishes a third article by Mohamud. This piece, also written under his pen name, examines jihadi media.

August 31, 2009: Amro al-Ali, a Saudi Arabian, emails his friend Mohamud from Yemen. He sends information about an Islamic school in that Middle East nation. The U.S. government considers the leader of the school a terrorist. That same day, Mohamud's dad phones the FBI in Portland, Oregon. He tells an agent that he believes his son has been radicalized by Muslim extremists and that he plans to fly to Yemen to fight against America. The FBI soon opens an investigation of Mohamud.

Fall 2009: Mohamud moves to Corvallis, Oregon, to begin studies at Oregon State University. FBI agents in Portland turn over the case to a team of investigators in Eugene, Oregon. Agents are now secretly reading all of Mohamud's emails.

November 9, 2009: Mohamud receives the first of many emails from "Bill Smith," who seeks his advice on how to attack the United States and its allies. Mohamud, wary of Smith, warns him to be careful because there are "spies" out there. Indeed, "Smith" is an informant for the FBI.

December 2009: Amro al-Ali writes to Mohamud, saying he is in Mecca, Saudi Arabia, the holiest place in the Muslim world. But the FBI learns that al-Ali is lying. He is in Yemen, a cradle of al-Qaeda. Al-Ali sends Mohamud the email address of a terrorist brother who can help him get overseas. Mohamud attempts to reach the man, but fails.

June 14, 2010: Mohamud goes to Portland International Airport to fly to Alaska for a summer job. But security officials tell him he cannot fly. The FBI has put him on its No Fly List because of his possible ties to terrorists. Two FBI agents interview Mohamud and his bewildered parents. Mohamud does not tell them that he wants to go to Yemen to fight against America.

June 23, 2010: An undercover FBI agent using the name Youssef emails Mohamud. He urges Mohamud to open a private email account on Hushmail. Mohamud responds from his new Hushmail account.

Late June 2010: Youssef and Mohamud continue their email exchange. Mohamud tells Youssef he was betrayed by his family and forced to stay in the U.S., but that he wants to go overseas. Mohamud makes plans to meet Youssef in Portland.

July 30, 2010: Mohamud and Youssef meet in downtown Portland. The two men walk to a hotel. Youssef explains that he is a recruiter for al-Qaeda. Mohamud tells him that he wants to take part in a truck bombing. Youssef tells him he might know someone who could build such a bomb.

August 19, 2010: Mohamud meets Youssef and his friend "Hussein" at the Portland hotel. Hussein is an undercover FBI operative. He pretends to be an explosives expert for al-Qaeda. Mohamud reveals that he wants to drive a truck bomb into Portland's annual Christmas tree-lighting celebration at Pioneer Courthouse Square.

September 7, 2010: Mohamud meets again with Youssef and Hussein. They worry he might team up with someone else in a terrorist attack. They tell him that they do not want him to commit a suicide bombing. Mohamud agrees. Hussein gives him a list of electronics to buy—including two Nokia cell phones—to build their bomb.

September 30, 2010: The FBI receives a box of bomb components that Mohamud has mailed to Hussein.

October 3, 2010: Mohamud meets Hussein and Youssef in a hotel room in Corvallis. He draws them a map of Pioneer Courthouse Square. The undercover agents ask Mohamud to rent a large storage facility for their truck bomb.

November 4, 2010: Youssef and Hussein pick up Mohamud in Corvallis. They drive deep into Oregon's coastal mountains. There, Mohamud dials a cell phone number thinking it will detonate a small test bomb. Behind the scenes, the FBI sets off the explosive. Later, Mohamud dresses up like Osama bin Laden to videotape his warning to America.

November 18, 2010: Mohamud takes Youssef and Hussein to the storage space he has rented in Corvallis. He presents them with keys to the space. They ride to Portland, where Mohamud shows them the parking space at Pioneer Courthouse Square that he has picked for the truck bomb.

November 23, 2010: Hussein picks up Mohamud in Corvallis and they visit the storage facility. There, Hussein shows Mohamud parts for the bomb he is building. This includes metal screws that Hussein says will shoot from the bomb like bullets. Hussein asks Mohamud to purchase another toggle switch.

November 26, 2010: Mohamud meets Youssef and Hussein at a waterfront hotel in Portland. The undercover operatives show Mohamud a huge bomb in a white van. It is a harmless fake. Later they park the van next to

Pioneer Courthouse Square. Thousands of people gather in the square for the city's annual Christmas tree lighting. Mohamud and Hussein make their way to a distant parking lot, where Mohamud twice dials a cell phone to detonate what he believes is a live bomb. A team of FBI agents jump out of a nearby van and arrest him.

November 29, 2010: A federal grand jury in Portland indicts Mohamud on a single charge: attempted use of a weapon of mass destruction.

January 10, 2013: Trial begins in the case of *USA v. Mohamud.*

January 31, 2013: A seven-woman, five-man jury in United States District Court finds Mohamud guilty of attempting to use a weapon of mass destruction on the night of Portland's Christmas tree-lighting ceremony.

October 1, 2014: A senior federal judge sentences Mohamud to thirty years in prison.

What Is a Sting Operation?

One of the FBI's many investigative techniques is the sting.

In a sting operation, sly agents (or their informants) go undercover. They pose as criminals to befriend suspected lawbreakers. Targets of a sting often welcome new friends as partners in crime. Secretly, agents collect evidence against them. Their undercover work, which sometimes drags on for months, is similar to acting in films. But FBI agents don't win Oscars for their best performances. They send criminals to prison.

Many police agencies conduct stings. For example, police officers or their informants pose as drug addicts to buy dangerous narcotics from street dealers. The undercover buyers turn the drugs over to detectives, who sweep in to arrest the dealers.

In the terrorism sting against Mohamed Mohamud, two FBI operatives pretended to be al-Qaeda terrorists.

They met with the teenager many times during their five-month sting operation. When they found out that Mohamud wanted to set off a bomb at a public gathering in Portland, Oregon, they tested him repeatedly to see if he was serious. Indeed, agents discovered, Mohamud was deadly serious.

The FBI arrested Mohamud on November 26, 2010, after he dialed a cell phone—twice—that he thought would detonate a massive bomb.

How This Book
Was Written

I filled many notebooks with details and observations about the Mohamed Mohamud case while working as a reporter for *The Oregonian* newspaper in Portland. Later, I reviewed many volumes of paper files, including notes I took at Mohamud's three-week trial.

Those volumes included:

- Several thousand pages of court records
- The trial transcript (about three thousand pages)
- Hundreds of trial exhibits, including surveillance photos, emails, jihadi literature, contracts, and receipts
- Interviews with key figures in the Mohamud case, including FBI investigators, prosecutors, defense lawyers, terrorism experts, and trial witnesses
- Print and broadcast news accounts from *The Oregonian*, *The New York Times*, *Salon*, *The Wall Street Journal*, Oregon Public Broadcasting, and other news organizations.

I conducted long in-person interviews with two key characters in the story—Special Agent Ryan Dwyer and Special Agent Miltiadis Trousas—and followed up with them through rounds of fact checking. I also interviewed retired FBI supervisor Nancy Savage, Assistant U.S. Attorney Ethan D. Knight, and former U.S. Attorney Dwight C. Holton. Two other agents—Elvis Chan and John Hallock—provided details and insights by email.

Many authors of nonfiction books, including investigative reporters like me, create chronologies of the most compelling events in their stories. I punched every solid detail I learned about the case into an Excel spreadsheet, which provided a searchable blow-by-blow account.

That timeline served as the backbone of this story.

KEY ARABIC WORDS AND PHRASES IN THIS BOOK

al-Qaeda: a terrorist group co-founded by Osama bin Laden. Al-Qaeda was responsible for the attacks of September 11, 2001.

Alhamdulillah: praise be to God

Allahu akbar: God is great

hadith: a Muslim religious text

hajj: pilgrimage

inshallah: if God wills it

jihad: a struggle, fight, or war against the enemies of Islam; also, a person's spiritual struggle against sin

mujahideen: Muslim guerrillas who wage violent jihad

mutafajirat: explosives

Quran: the Islamic holy book

Shahada: the declaration of faith in Islam: "there is no god but Allah, and Muhammad is the messenger of Allah."

Sources

News Articles

January 11, 2002: Warraq, Ibn. "Virgins? What virgins?" *The Guardian.*

February 11, 2003: Minaya, Zeke. "Jury Calls for Execution of Gang Member Who Killed 4 in Nightclub." *Los Angeles Times.*

January 8, 2010: Coker, Margaret. "Yemen Ties Alleged Attacker to al Qaeda and U.S.-Born Cleric." *The Wall Street Journal.*

January 13, 2010: Ghosh, Bobby. "How Dangerous Is the Cleric Anwar al-Awlaki?" *Time.*

January 18, 2010: Erlanger, Steven. "At Yemen College, Scholarship and Jihadist Ideas." *The New York Times.*

October 12, 2010: Ryan, Jason. "'I Am Proud to Be A Traitor to America,' Boasts American al Qaeda." *ABC News.*

November 27, 2010: Denson, Bryan. "FBI Thwarts Terrorist Bombing Attempt at Portland Holiday Tree Lighting, Authorities Say." *The Oregonian.*

November 28, 2010: Cole, Gail; Jonathan Cooper and
Nigel Duara. "Mosque Target of Arson, Possible Hate
Crime." *Corvallis Gazette-Times, The Associated Press.*

November 29, 2010: Denson, Bryan. "Accused Portland
Bomb Plotter Mohamed Mohamud Pleads Not
Guilty; Attorneys Raise Entrapment Issue." *The
Oregonian.*

November 29, 2010: Yardley, William. "Entrapment Is
Argued in Defense of Suspect." *The New York Times.*

December 5, 2010: Terry, Lynne. "Family of Portland's
Bomb Suspect, Mohamed Mohamud, Fled Chaos in
Somalia for New Life in America." *The Oregonian.*

June 2, 2011: Denson, Bryan. "Bomb Case Defense
Zeroes In on Battery." *The Oregonian.*

August 26, 2011: Duara, Nigel. "Documents reveal rantings
of mosque fire suspect." The Associated Press.

September 9, 2011: Berger, J. M. "Anwar Al-Awlaki's
Links to the September 11 Hijackers." *The Atlantic.*

September 29, 2011: Greenwald, Glenn. "The FBI Again
Thwarts Its Own Terror Plot." *Salon.*

September 30, 2011: Fordham, Alice. "A 'Proud Traitor':
Samir Khan Reported Dead Alongside Aulaqi." *The
Washington Post.*

September 30, 2011: Brown, Robbie, and Kim, Severson. "2nd American in Strike Waged Qaeda Media War." *The New York Times.*

October 1, 2011: Almasmari, Hakim; Margaret Coker and Siobhan Gorman. "Drone Kills Top Al Qaeda Figure." *The Wall Street Journal.*

November 25, 2011: Denson, Bryan. "Portland Bomb Sting, One Year Later." *The Oregonian.*

April 18, 2012: Denson, Bryan. "Mohamud to Receive FBI Info." *The Oregonian.*

March 22, 2012: Goode, Erica. "Stronger Hand for Judges in the 'Bazaar' of Plea Deals." *The New York Times.*

March 22, 2012: Denson, Bryan. "Bomb-Plot Suspect's Case Centers on Emails." *The Oregonian.*

May 2, 2012: Denson, Bryan. "Mohamud's Dad Called FBI, Agent Testifies." *The Oregonian.*

September 25, 2012: Denson, Bryan. "Defense in Bomb Trial Takes Issue with FBI's Actions at PDX Run-In." *The Oregonian.*

September 26, 2012: Denson, Bryan. "Portland Judge Rules Terrorism Suspect Mohamud Can't Learn True Identity of FBI Informant." *The Oregonian.*

October 24, 2012: Denson, Bryan. "Mohamud Was to Flee to Yemen, Filings Say." *The Oregonian.*

October 29, 2012: Denson, Bryan. "Mohamud Lawyers Key In on Wording." *The Oregonian.*

November 28, 2012: Denson, Bryan. "Hidden Identities at Trial OK'd." *The Oregonian.*

November 30, 2012: Denson, Bryan. "Psychologists: Suspect Plied by Feds with Flattery." *The Oregonian.*

January 9, 2013: Staff of *The Oregonian.* "Portland Terrorism Trial: Chief Defense Attorney Stephen Sady a Longtime Challenger of Government's Use of Power."

January 9, 2013: Denson, Bryan. "Portland Terrorism Trial: Lead Prosecutor Ethan Knight a Self-Deprecating Workaholic with High-Profile Portfolio." *The Oregonian.*

January 9, 2013: Denson, Bryan. "Portland Terrorism Trial: Mohamud Faces Long Odds with Entrapment Defense, Good Chance of Favorable Jury." *The Oregonian.*

January 10, 2013: Denson, Bryan. "Portland Terrorism Trial: Opening Statements Expected Friday in Mohamed Mohamud Case." *The Oregonian.*

January 11, 2013: Denson, Bryan. "Portland Terrorism Trial: Was Mohamed Mohamud a Committed Jihadist or a Goofy Kid?" *The Oregonian.*

January 12, 2013: Denson, Bryan. "Mohamud: Wildly Different Portraits." *The Oregonian.*

January 14, 2013: Denson, Bryan. "Portland Terrorism Trial: FBI Agent Says Mohamed Mohamud Corresponded with 'Dangerous People.'" *The Oregonian.*

January 15, 2013: Denson, Bryan. "FBI Agent Tells How He Courted Mohamud." *The Oregonian.*

January 16, 2013: Denson, Bryan. "Portland Terrorism Trial: Undercover Agents Treated Mohamed Mohamud Like Son, Defense Suggests." *The Oregonian.*

January 16, 2013: Denson, Bryan. "Mohamud's 'Goodbye' Shown at Trial." *The Oregonian.*

January 17, 2013: Denson, Bryan. "Recording Was Made of Practice Bombing." *The Oregonian.*

January 18, 2013: Denson, Bryan. "Defense Team Grills FBI Agents over Plot." *The Oregonian.*

January 18, 2013: Denson, Bryan. "Portland Terrorism Trial: Testimony, Tapes Give Clearest Account So Far of Final Hours of Bomb Plot." *The Oregonian.*

January 19, 2013: Denson, Bryan. "Mohamud's Actions on Tree-Lighting Day Retold." *The Oregonian.*

January 23, 2013: Denson, Bryan. "Portland Terrorism

Trial: FBI Agents Trace Trail That Led Them to Mohamed Mohamud." *The Oregonian.*

January 24, 2013: Denson, Bryan. "FBI Spent Months Tailing Mohamud and Assessing Him." *The Oregonian.*

January 24, 2013: Denson, Bryan. "Portland Terrorism Trial: FBI Agent Recounts Scores of Mohamed Mohamud Emails to Suspected Terrorists." *The Oregonian.*

January 25, 2013: Baer, April. "Mohamud Trial: Botched Recording Takes Center Stage in Court." Oregon Public Broadcasting, opb.org/news/series/mohamud /mohamud-trial-botched-recording-takes-center -stage-in-court.

January 25, 2013: Denson, Bryan. "In Trial, Talk of Allah and Beer Pong." *The Oregonian.*

January 25, 2013: Denson, Bryan. "Portland Terrorism Trial: Before His Arrest, Mohamed Mohamud Kept Saying 'I Love You Guys' to Friends." *The Oregonian.*

January 25, 2013: Denson, Bryan. "Portland Terrorism Trial: Mohamed Mohamud Showed Key Signs of Violent Jihad Tendencies, Expert Says." *The Oregonian.*

January 26, 2013: Denson, Bryan. "Mohamud Showed Key Danger Signs, Expert Says." *The Oregonian.*

January 28, 2013: Denson, Bryan. "Portland Terrorism Trial: 'This Is Bad . . . Mohamed's Been Arrested,' Parents Recall." *The Oregonian.*

January 29, 2013: Denson, Bryan. "Portland Terrorism Trial: Mohamed Mohamud's Cover Story For Foreign Travel? Rap Artist." *The Oregonian.*

January 29, 2013: Denson, Bryan. "Parents Worried for Mohamud." *The Oregonian.*

January 30, 2013: Denson, Bryan. "Portland Terrorism Trial: 'This Case Is a Tragedy,' Mohamed Mohamud's Lawyer Says." *The Oregonian.*

January 30, 2013: Denson, Bryan. "Witnesses Label Mohamud Immature." *The Oregonian.*

January 31, 2013: Denson, Bryan. "A 'Tragedy' or a Tragedy Averted?" *The Oregonian.*

January 31, 2013: Denson, Bryan. "Mohamed Mohamud Found Guilty in Portland Terrorism Trial." *The Oregonian.*

February 1, 2013: Denson, Bryan. "Jury Sees Terrorist, Not Victim." *The Oregonian.*

February 2, 2013: Denson, Bryan. "Mohamed Mohamud's Lawyers Will Challenge Secrecy

Surrounding Key Witnesses in Portland Terrorism Trial." *The Oregonian.*

February 3, 2013: Denson, Bryan. "The Right to Face One's Accusers: An Appeal for Mohamed Mohamud Is Likely to Focus on Secret Identities of the Testifying Agents." *The Oregonian.*

March 9, 2013: Mazzetti, Mark; Charlie Savage and Scott Shane. "How a U.S. Citizen Came to Be in America's Cross Hairs." *The New York Times.*

June 9, 2013: Denson, Bryan. "Mohamud Is Likely to Get Decades in Prison." *The Oregonian.*

October 16, 2013: Savage, Charlie. "Door May Open for Challenge to Secret Wiretaps." *The New York Times.*

October 21, 2013: Denson, Bryan. "AG Loretta Lynch presents Mohamed Mohamud Prosecution Team with National Security Award." *The Oregonian.*

November 19, 2013: Denson, Bryan. "Portland Bomb Plot: Government Used Warrantless Wiretaps Overseas that Helped Make Case Against Mohamud." *The Oregonian.*

October 1, 2014: Jung, Helen. "Mohamud Bomb Plot: Unwavering Commitment to Terrorism Plan

Earned 30-Year Sentence, Judge Says." *The Oregonian*

September 16, 2015: Denson, Bryan. "Mohamed Mohamud files formal appeal, sets stage for US surveillance program showdown." *The Oregonian*.

March 2, 2016: Bruttell, Nathan. "Man Convicted of Firebombing Corvallis Mosque Gets Probation." *Corvallis Gazette-Times*.

September 23, 2016: O'Haver, Hanson. "How 'If You See Something, Say Something' Became Our National Motto." *The Washington Post*.

December 5, 2016: Savage, Charlie. "Terrorism Convicton of a Wiretapped American Is Upheld on Appeal." *The New York Times*.

March 1, 2017: CNN Library. "Anwar al-Awlaki Fast Facts." *CNN World*.

March 7, 2017: Miner, Colin. "Trump Travel Ban Won't Keep Us Safe, Says US Attorney Who Prosecuted Would-Be Bomber." *Patch*.

November 12, 2018: CNN Library. "Mumbai Terror Attacks Fast Facts." *CNN*.

February 6, 2019: Wong, Peter. "Garr King, former federal judge, dies." *Portland Tribune*.

March 9, 2019: Barrett, Devlin. "Arrests in Domestic
Terror Probes Outpace Those Inspired by Islamic
Extremists." *The Washington Post.*

Key Court Records and Executive Order

November 26, 2010: Criminal Complaint and Affidavit,
*United States of America v. Mohamed Osman
Mohamud,* U.S. District Court, District of Oregon.

November 29, 2010: Indictment of Mohamed Osman
Mohamud, *United States of America v. Mohamed
Osman Mohamud,* U.S. District Court, District of
Oregon.

January–February 2013: Trial transcript, *United States of
America v. Mohamed Osman Mohamud,* U.S. District
Court, District of Oregon.

September 4, 2015: Opening Brief of Appellant, Appeal
from the U.S. District Court for the District of
Oregon.

December 5, 2016: Opinion, *United States of America v.
Mohamed Osman Mohamud,* U.S. Court of Appeals
for the Ninth Circuit.

March 6, 2017: Trump, President Donald J., Executive
Order Protecting the Nation from Foreign Terrorist
Entry into the United States.

Press Releases

June 15, 2009: FBI National Press Releases. "Arthur Balizan Named Special Agent in Charge of Portland Division."

November 26, 2010: Holton, Dwight C., U.S. Attorney. "Oregon Resident Arrested in Plot to Bomb Christmas Tree Lighting Ceremony in Portland: Vehicle Bomb Left at Scene Was Inert and Posed No Danger to Public."

February 4, 2011: U.S. Attorney's Office, Northern District of California. "Gang Leader Sentenced to 13 Consecutive Terms of Life Imprisonment: Anh The Duong Previously Found Guilty of Murdering Four People During Armed Robberies or Attempted Armed Robberies in Aid of Racketeering."

October 21, 2015: U.S. Attorney's Office, District of Oregon. "12 Individuals in District of Oregon Receive Attorney General Awards."

Studies, Reports, and Scholarly Papers

Bacastow, Todd S.; Patrick Biltgen, Thom Kaye, and Jeffrey M. Young. "Activity-Based Intelligence:

Understanding Patterns-of-Life." *The State and Future of GEOINT 2017*, United States Geospatial Intelligence Foundation, 2017. pp. 24–27.

Cook, David. "Martyrdom (Shahada)." Oxford Bibliographies. n.d.

Felter, Claire; Jonathan Masters and Mohammed Aly Sergie. "Al-Shabab." Council on Foreign Relations, 2019. cfr.org/backgrounder/al-shabab.

Franz, Nina. "Targeted Killing and Pattern-of-Life Analysis: Weaponised Media." *Media, Culture & Society* (special issue: The Media and the Military), vol. 39, no. 1, pp. 111–21, 2017.

Hackett, Conrad and David McClendon. "Christians Remain World's Largest Religious Group, but They Are Declining in Europe." *FactTank: News in the Numbers*, Pew Research Center, Apr. 5, 2017. pewresearch.org/fact-tank/2017/04/05/christians -remain-worlds-largest-religious-group-but-they-are -declining-in-europe.

Human Rights Watch, "Yemen Events of 2018." *World Report 2019*. hrw.org/world-report/2019/country -chapters/yemen.

Moghadam, Assaf: "The Salafi-Jihad as a Religious

Ideology." *CTC Sentinel*, vol. 1, no. 3, 2008. ctc.usma
.edu/the-salafi-jihad-as-a-religious-ideology.

Books

Encyclopedia of Modern Worldwide Extremists and
Extremist Groups. Atkins, Stephen E. Westport, CT.
Greenwood, 2004.

ACKNOWLEDGMENTS

Writing is lonely business, but good writing involves a crowd.

I'm grateful to the crowd of fine people who helped make this book possible. First among them is Kristin (Quinlan) Denson, my longtime love, who made me an honest man by marrying me during the writing of this book. While I'm skeptical of the existence of muses (those goddesses said to spark creative genius in us mortals), Kristin's love, good humor, and belief in me is a constant source of inspiration. And I am madly in love with her.

I owe a galaxy of thanks to all the FBI agents who graciously answered my questions about the Mohamud case. I'm especially indebted to agents Ryan Dwyer and Miltiadis Trousas, whose insights and expertise made my job so much easier. Their recall of events in this story was often jaw-dropping. Special thanks also go to agents

Elvis Chan and John Hallock, and to former agent Nancy Savage, who once headed the FBI's Eugene, Oregon, office and now serves as executive director of the Society of Former Special Agents of the FBI.

Many thanks also to Assistant U.S. Attorney Ethan D. Knight, chief prosecutor in *USA v. Mohamud*, for his thoughtful words about the criminal case and the trial, and his willingness to share his expertise on national security law.

I'm deeply indebted to three FBI employees who spend their days helping journalists. Beth Anne Steele, the FBI's public affairs officer in Portland, arranged multiple interviews with agents in two Oregon cities and served as an intermediary as I checked facts with those agents by email. Christopher Allen and Shelley Wilson, in the Investigative Publicity and Public Affairs Unit at FBI headquarters, have helped me throughout my work on the FBI Files series.

As always, I am eternally grateful to my superb agent, Tamar Rydzinski at Context Literary Agency, for encouraging me to write the FBI Files series and helping me navigate the publishing world for the last seven years. A zillion thanks to Katherine Jacobs, my editor at Roaring Brook Press, whose skillful editing—aimed at keeping younger readers turning the pages—has made this series a great success. I must also thank two other Roaring Brook employees—copyeditor Nancy Elgin and assistant editor Luisa Beguiristain—for their expert reads of this manuscript.

INDEX